Why Aren't You Writing?

Unlocking Your Potential to Write Books
It is Your Season, Your Destiny!

A handbook created and designed with you in mind

Carol S. Batey, Ph.D.

Author of *Parents Are Lifesavers, In Due Season, Poise for the Runway of Your Life, & What's Cooking in Your Soul?*

Are you ready to unlock and unleash your creativity? YOU hold the key! This book will guide you into the world of writing your books. You will become the embodied entrepreneur writer that you know you should be. Write ON!

CENTERING PRESS
an imprint of Westry Wingate Group, Inc.

Westry Wingate Group, Inc.
http://www.wwgpress.com

ISBN-13: 978-1-935323-10-5
ISBN-10: 1-935323-10-5

Why Aren't You Writing?

CENTERING
PRESS

I Am Grateful

So many people cross your path in life and leave their footprints on your soul. The Rev. Alice J. Brown, Senior Minister of Living Truth Center for Better Living, East Cleveland, Ohio, has been more than a friend to me; she has been my angel of inspirational guidance. This project, my books, as well as my classes on "how to write books" were her ideas. There is a chapter in my fourth book entitled "Why Aren't You Writing?" Yet, everywhere I went to speak or teach, the one question that resonated above all others was "how do you write a book?" Last year, I hosted a radio program on a Christian station and that same question was again asked of me. It took the Rev. Brown to open my eyes; to see that this was a needed task for those who wanted to learn "how to write books." I honor her spiritual insights and wisdom.

I am grateful to Doris Bush, my proof reader; to my editors Lydia Cox and Mindy Liska; to David Dickerson, my graphic artist; to Ramiah Branch, my photographer and artistic director; to Fred Finch, my web presence developer; to Emily Heinlen, my researcher and virtual assistant; and lastly, to Lolita Pride, who, without her expertise and advice, this project would not have been possible.

When you are working on a project, there are voices that push you along the way: Carolyn Parker, Gloria Sawyers, Hilda Shrunk, and all my writing students. This book is for all the writing students who will embrace it's teaching.

Westry Wingate Group & the Centering Press imprint, to whom I am grateful, make this book possible.

Thank you, God, Infinite Wisdom and Love, for the ability to create textbooks for people who have desires to create and tell their stories, non-fiction or fiction.

Namaste.

About the Author

Carol S. Batey, Ph.D. author of Parents Are Lifesavers (Corwin Press 1996), In Due Season: Destiny's Calling Your Soul (AuthorHouse 2007), Poise for the Runway of Your Life (AuthorHouse 2009), What's Cooking in Your Soul? (AuthorHouse 2010), and Why Aren't You Writing? (Westry Wingate 2011), is committed to sharing information about how one can improve and renew the purpose of one's soul. Carol provides coaching workshops and seminars for anyone who desires to step into their destiny.

Carol has received a Doctoral degree in Metaphysics, at the University of Metaphysics at the University of Sedona. Carol has worked as a Parent Involvement Consultant for the Metropolitan Nashville (Tennessee) Public Schools and received national recognition from educators for her work on parent involvement. During the 1992 school year, she was nominated for the J.C. Penney Golden Rule Award, an award given to individuals who have performed outstanding service to the local community, and the school won $1,000. Over the past seventeen years, Carol has appeared on TV, radio, internet, national radio programs, as well as in newsprint.

Carol, born and raised in Nashville, Tennessee, is the mother of six adult children and the author of numerous magazine, newspaper articles, as well as YouTube videos. Carol was educated in the Nashville Public Schools system, and has obtained multiple Associate Degrees in business from various schools in Nashville. She is also a visual artist and the creator of her own skin care line.

Carol, at 51, is a Lifestyle Model for Elite Models in Atlanta and a talent of Sharon Smith Talent. She has worked in the performing arts on various assignments. Her "Your Destiny Awaits You" and "Hold on to Your Dreams" workshops are very popular, and attendees leave with knowledge, motivation, and instruction, as well as a sense of self-empowerment. Her signature class is "Why Aren't You Writing?"

She welcomes your e-mails or personal calls for speaking, coaching, retreats, or workshops for your organization or yourself. Contact Carol via carol37076@aol.com; (615)-485-4548; or her website: www.artlifestylecoach.com; find her on Facebook or on her blog, www.carolsbatey.blogspot.com

Dedication

This handbook is a celebration of my work for you, the reader. I kept you in my heart, mind, and soul as I wrote to you, my dear. Everything under this Earth is spiritual. Now, celebrate your writing! My goal is for you to become an entrepreneur writer and make a living in this craft. This book is yours.

You will learn the following: how to get ready to write, how to put a plan into place, gain motivation, learn who your target audience is, how to organize your thoughts, when to rewrite, refine and polish your works, copyright, market and social network, find editing support, handle rejections, find a literary agent, create query letters, publishers and more.

– Author Carol S. Batey

Let Nothing Disturb Thee

Let nothing disturb you, nothing frighten you,
All things are passing, God never changes,
Patient endurance will attain to all things;
Who God possesses, in nothing is wanting;
Alone God suffices.

~St. Teresa of Avila (1515-1582)

~Table of Contents~

Table of Contents

Introduction
Why Aren't You Writing?

"One writes to teach, to move or to delight."
~Rodolphus Agricola (1444-1485)

This workbook has been designed to unleash the writer within you! You have the key and the dedication that unlocks your writing potential. Can you use it? Within this workbook, I share insights, challenges, and skills that I have gained from writing and publishing for the past fifteen years. Are you ready to write your book? Can you go to bed early, wake up around 2 a.m. and write? Can you get up early to write? Choose a time that works for you. **Do you have a book that's unwritten within your soul?** What is keeping you from writing it? When will you start the writing process? Do you want to write for your own personal enjoyment, to give direction for others, or to be published? Some people write to leave a legacy for their children. I write for all these important reasons! Are you one of those waiting to be motivated or inspired? Maybe you are afraid that by committing your ideas to paper, others will be able to see your vulnerabilities. Perhaps you are afraid that you will not have enough time to commit to the project. Are you letting your lack of computer skills hold you back? Do you perceive yourself as having a lack of formal education? Do you lack confidence in yourself as I once did? Why do **you** want to write? What can you release in order to step into your destiny to write books? For me, I go to bed between 6:30 and 8:00 p.m. and when Spirit awakens me to write around 2 a.m., I get up and write. I then start my day at 6:30 a.m.

Have you had dreams of writing a book? On many occasions, I have dreamt that I was in a corner writing a book. Then, I dreamt that I was holding my third published book and shaking all over. I dreamt about the cover of my third book with the title in gold and my name standing out.

In seventeen years, I have written and published five books and numerous articles. My specialized knowledge now is for your benefit, to learn. I freely share this with you, dear writer. God has blessed me with the ability to tap into "Infinite Wisdom" in order to write these books. In return, I have trusted the unseen powers of God to help and guide me without question. My inspiration to write comes solely and directly from God. Spirit has also provided others along the way to help me in areas in which I needed assistance. These individuals helped me to reach my ultimate potential. I am obedient to Spirit's call to write. During the process of writing books, I realized that I needed additional assistance. Therefore, I placed an ad on various websites on the Internet, asking for assistance and immediately received the help I needed.

Each book is different, and I know that I have had Divine angels assisting me along the way. In order to accept help from the angels and God, you must understand and accept that Divine Guidance is directing and operating in your life as you write. If you are one who questions your abilities and lives in a sea of doubt, do not allow these thoughts to cloud your ambitions any longer. In times of doubt, I often turn to Ralph Waldo Trine. His book, *In Tune with the Infinite*, is one that I often find inspiring and helpful:

> "When one becomes thoroughly individualized, he enters into the realm of all knowledge and wisdom; and to be individualized is to recognize no power outside of the Infinite Power that is back of all. When one recognizes this great fact and opens himself to this Spirit of Infinite Wisdom, he then enters upon the road to the true education, and mysteries that before were closed now reveal themselves to him. This must indeed be the foundation of all true education, this evolving from within, this evolving of what has been involved by the Infinite Power." (1897, p. 100)

I know that this handbook will be the key that will unleash the writer within you **today**! Will you turn the key within your soul and start to write today?

Blessings, Carol S. Batey (entrepreneur/author)

Chapter 1
The Beginning of Carol's Writing

"I have written so much about me because I am the subject on whom I am the best informed."
~Samuel Butler (1835-1902)

Everyone has a beginning of how they started to write. Some have written in journals since children and that process has carried on into adulthood. What is your starting point? My story demonstrates how God directs our lives as we commit to step into God's plans. Thus, I am the best informed on me – how about you?

My first book: *Parents Are Lifesavers* (1996)

I volunteered at my younger children's school, which was located in the inner city in a drug-infested neighborhood in Nashville. The children were bused into the area from their home districts. The principal asked me to be the Parent/Teacher Club President, and having such a leadership position at the school proved to be a joyful, enlightening, and rewarding experience. After my first year, I was nominated for and won a J.C. Penney Leadership Award. Soon after, other local schools began calling for my help and leadership. At first, I answered these calls free of charge, but soon, I realized that what I thought was my hobby was actually a calling from God.

One day, I attended a special development meeting for a new director of the Metropolitan Nashville Public School System. As he spoke, I wrote down notes and altered his philosophies and insights to fit my thoughts on how parents should be involved in their children's schools. The director continued to speak at several of these open forums. I took my turn to stand in line for the microphone and explained what I had initiated concerning parental involvement at my child's school. At the end of this forum, the director came up to me and told me that he enjoyed my comments. I told him that he should offer me a job. His response was that there were not any jobs available with a job description to fit my qualifications. I said to him, "Dr. Benjamin, you are the school's director. You can create a job for me. Shall I make an appointment to come and see you?" That is how I created my job and was able to write the book, Parents Are Lifesavers! It should be noted that the position created by the school's director and myself was without an advanced degree, but only with the information that I gathered as a volunteer and information learned after I was hired. It was the start of a wonderful career and a unique way to create a life for myself outside of my home. Up until that point, I was known strictly as a wife and a stay-at-home mom of six children. To accomplish this project, I got up at three a.m. to write. This was while my husband worked the night shift and before my six children got up.

Remember, this new career started with a simple volunteer position and a desire to help others. However, the turning point was when I committed the ideas that God had given me to paper in the form of the handbook for other schools. What are you willing to commit to create your book?

___

___

___

Persistence Pays Off

One must exercise and practice persistence when designing your life, world, and affairs. As a parental consultant working for the school district, I needed to create a parental consultant brochure to define the mission of my new job. I was allowed to attend three conferences a year. At each conference, I collected business cards from those in attendance who worked in education. After going through every address that I had of people who specialized in education, I sent them a copy of the brochure. One of these contacts was a major education publisher, Corwin Press. Within three weeks, I received a phone call from the company asking me if I would be interested in developing a handbook on parental involvement for teachers, parent leaders, and administrators. The acquisition editor told me that they usually ask professors to write such books, but they wanted a "parent who had been there" to share her insights instead. Once I got over the shock, I accepted the assignment; I had to write a proposal for the book! I began writing a handbook for the schools in my area who called for my advice.

Writing with the Infinite

At this time, in 1994, I did not have a computer, nor did I know how to use one. I decided to ask God for help, which is the first step in all things. By using and tapping into the "Infinite Wisdom," I was led to a personal editor who I hired to help me clean up and type my writing. You can find similar help in writing magazines, at colleges, or online such as HireMyMom.com. I will give more advice on this topic later. By trusting in God, I have always been supplied with the help that I needed, and you can be too. Can you, my dears, trust God that all will be supplied according to your needs for writing?

After the proposal, I received the contract. Next, I turned to my personal editor to help me with the book. I still did not own a computer, so I handwrote the entire book. Once I had finished a chapter, I would mail it to my Corwin Press editor, who would call me after she received it to discuss and revise the contents. After making the necessary changes, she would mail back the manuscript. This process continued for eight months.

This process of critique is one of the most challenging to a writer. Once they reviewed the chapter, Corwin Press would send me their assessment and critique. In such a process, you must always stay open to the views of others, especially those who are professionals in the writing business. You must trust them and keep your mind open so that you can learn from them. It is important to keep your mind open to constructive criticism, no matter how hard it may be to hear.

Do not take any criticism personally. It is merely meant to help you improve.

Often people who write are told to never write about themselves; however, you are the only story you know very well. Try to balance the first person (that is you) that you are writing about. When the book was completed, the publishing company sent it to a professor in my home town of Nashville for review. His response was that it was missing my personal story. The editor from Corwin Press then called me to tell me that I needed to include my personal story in the book. At first, I was angry because I thought they wanted me to focus only on theory. Nevertheless, I did not stay mad for long as I had a job to do!

Being Tapped on the Shoulder

As I slept in my bed at midnight, I felt someone tap me on my shoulder. I looked around, but no one was there. I heard a voice say, "Get up and write." I got up and handwrote my personal story for the next twelve hours for *Parents Are Lifesavers;* that became the first chapter of that book.

Summary

As you can see, I faced limitations and had to do things beyond my own ability. Yet, I sought the Infinite Wisdom of the Almighty God. God is my source and strength and within that knowledge, I can do all things that I am called to do, and that means writing as well!

Re-read this chapter of my very beginning – the start of my legacy to create books. Take notes, meditate, and ponder how you will start. If you are one who has already started publishing, it is my hope that you will gain further insight from my writing path.

Meditation for Writers

"Writing is the entry point Spirit into matter."
~Bishop E. Bernard Jordan

Let the suggestion of fear go from our hearts, mind, and spirit. Let it float up and away from our soul into the atmosphere of nothing. If you believe God has called you to write a book, a grant, poems, or memories, answer the call by saying "YES" to God. Close your eyes and see the energy light in front of you reaching out to your soul and spirit. It is saying, "Follow me, my dear, on this path of writing. I will give you the words to put on the paper. You will have the wisdom from above and within your soul to influence and win others. You have some important insights and inspirations to share with others. Take the time to develop your skills. You can do it, you are my child.... You are made in the likeness and image of me.... All that I am you are...." Say "Yes." So be it!

MY THOUGHTS AND PRAYERS

"Thoughts unspoken are not unknown to the Divine Mind. Desire is prayer; and no loss can occur from trusting God with our desires, that they may be moulded and exalted before they take form in words and in deeds."

~Mary Baker Eddy, founder of Christian Science
(Science and Health with Key to the Scriptures, 1875, p. 1)

Take the time here to write down your thoughts. Remember, they are prayers as well.

Chapter 2
Your Starting Point

"All writing comes by the grace of God."
~Ralph Waldo Emerson (1803-1882)

The following passage is from my second book, *In Due Season: Destiny's Calling Your Soul* (2007). I have included this section for you to see and understand where I started as a writer, to communicate, and connect with my readers. Once you start your writing project, most of it will be done in solitude and by yourself with Spirit. Can you work alone with a Higher Power or Spirit? Most people who desire to write cannot be alone; they do not like the feeling of isolation.

> Dear Reader,
>
> While meditating, creating, and writing this book for you, I held you in my heart and mind. *In Due Season: Destiny is Calling Your Soul* is an account of my personal transformation and purpose on this Earth. The title *In Due Season* comes from the King James Bible, Galatians 6:9, "And let not us grow weary (give up) while doing well, for in (the right) time we shall reap (yield what we planted), if we do not lose heart (lose faith)."
>
> I put myself in your traveling shoes, covering the miles upon miles you will need to reach your ultimate inner goal or transformation. Many have asked how to identify the purpose of their journey. They have also asked how to make time to accomplish their purpose and where the money will come from. To uncover your personal transformation, you first start with a desire to create. Next, a spiritual practice of meditating, fasting and praying, journaling, being still and listening, attending a Center for Worship if you choose, as well as physical exercise and proper nutrition will assist you beginning on a spiritual and personal transformation.
>
> As I examined my ego, my true desires for the reasons for wanting change came out, and I made a commitment to do the hard work

necessary to get physically, spiritually, emotionally, and mentally fit. My goal was to become a new Carol. The labor and the miles traveled were not as hard once I surrendered and gave into the Universal Spirit's laws. The principles and applications in this book are tried, tested, and proven true if your mind, heart and soul are open and your spirit and mind are willing to do the hard work. I used them daily to achieve the desired results for my soul's purpose and personal transformation. Not every application may be for your soul's changes; think of what is needed for you.

With the Master Creator's divine help, we can awaken our minds, bodies, and souls to remember our purposes. Seeking the Divine's help by asking for assistance from Spirit is where we start, since we are co-creators of our destiny. Knocking down the walls of false ego and the barriers of protection we have built up over the years is second. Through a daily spiritual practice, you can gain courage, faith, inner well-being, insights, humility, directions and answers for your daily walk or journey. Surrendering helps one to lose the false ego that does not serve anyone but the ego. Humility is developed and welcomed, and then Spirit's help is there to guide you on your course. You and I become co-creators with the Divine God, our sacred source. God is a name that may be different for others. Trust in and gain wisdom from a Higher Power greater than yourself.

As spiritual beings on this Earth, you will face adverse conditions on your path, but do not look at the situation as right or wrong. Look past the objection and see the outcome you want to achieve. It is our earthly task to use our free will and discernment powers to move forward and not against the grain. Most problems are not as they appear.

This book will begin your awakening. If you allow it, you will find buried treasures within your soul, spirit, and mind. Principles mentioned will nourish and direct your soul. Then the power of God will start to transform your life. Spirit's guidance will be felt within your soul and around it, directing your path daily. Learn to let go, surrender to the Universal God and the Laws of the Earth - "The Law of Attraction and Allowing." You will inherit joy, peace, wisdom, abundant living, and a new purpose in life. You will create unity with your God.

Love and peace,

Carol S. Batey

Where Do Your Gifts Come From?

As we know, we all have gifts and talents that we have been blessed with from a Higher Power. Where do your gifts come from? Do they come from your job, a car, a bank account, or higher education? Can you write your book and tap into the inner wisdom from above? When it is time to answer the call to write, do you have inner doubts, fears, and concerns? Why is that so true? Take this time and write what comes up in your spirit about why you do not write.

____

____

____

____

____

____

____

____

How Do Those Feelings of Truth Look to You?

____

____

____

____

____

____

____

____

Can you see with your mind's eye how the things you **thought of as truth have affected you?** Now, whether they are true or not is the question at hand. Do you believe the concepts that you have told your mind repeatedly, and actually carried those messages out that played within your soul? When I knew I was going to write a book, long before Corwin Press called, I felt I did not have the smarts to really do it! My inner thoughts were that I could do it and at the same time, I could not. I had an inner war inside my soul; I was mentally and spiritually off-balance.

"Fear is nothing more than the negative use of faith."
~Ernest Holmes (1887-1960)

Limitations vs. Unlimited Wisdom

In the *Webster's New World Pocket Dictionary, limitation* is defined as "confined or setting limits on something." (p. 164) Do we set these limits upon ourselves and others because we are experiencing fear? In order to move from *fear* and practice *faith*, one must believe in a power higher than themselves and an unquestioning belief. This unquestioning belief could be in a religion, a Higher Power, and the confidence that you can do that to which you are called.

How many times have you and I faced inner limitations? However, it is what we decide to do with those limitations that determine who we are. I gain my source of strength to step into the desired destinies through the example of St. Teresa of Avila (1515-1582), a mystic and Roman Catholic nun. We all know of the dedication nuns exemplify with their walk and service to God. The bishops, to whom she reported, noticed that she had a unique relationship with God; one that they admired and respected. They instructed her to write about this relationship in order to help others in their relationships with God. They had inferior feelings for her abilities to tap into the powers of her Beloved for strength and power, yet they still put her writings and actions on trial. Once she proved herself to them that she was not of the devil, she wrote even for that hostile audience, the "learned ones." When assigned this important task, this wonderful teacher and writer questioned her capability to undertake it and felt that her lack of formal education and poor health would hinder her abilities. She felt that the responsibility should be undertaken by the "learned men" of the church. She soon developed her own mysticism and literary style; she would not meet her critic on their terms, but on hers alone. Often, she wrote so fast, wishing and hoping for six hands so that everything that came by inspiration could be written down. She was full of determination as we wrote, as she moved closer into the presence of Christ. She found her literacy voice and so can you! If she had not been able to be humble and accept the gifts provided to her by the Spirit, we would not have these writings today.

St. Teresa of Avila has been a guiding force within my life. I first came to know her by reading her stories and understanding the limitations she faced in her books, *Interior Castle* and *The Book of My Life.* When Teresa wrote my favorite, *Interior Castle* in 1577 at the age of 62, she had already written two other books. But by now she had come into full possession of her mysticism literary skills. As a writer, my dears, find your voice and stay true to yourself and have the determination. In order to move past your fears and what you feel about your limitations, you must have an unwavering inner faith and trust in God.

Opening Up Your Mind

People who aspire to write ask me over and over how to get started in writing books. They then ask me how I found inspiration and the time to write. Many want to understand the commitment to write books.

It all starts by opening your heart, mind, and spirit to receive information to put on paper or in a recording device. Observe your thoughts of what you are seeing and what you are surrounding yourself with. Are you overeating so much that you are too full and cannot hear the messages in your mind? For me, I started taking extra vitamins and an herb called ginkgo for memory alertness. Then, I applied meditation with prayer to get me grounded.

Here is My Plan of Action - Adapt This for Yourself:

1. Ask God for assistance, direction, and wisdom to write and then surrender to that Living, Loving Spirit. Maybe you do not know a power higher than yourself; can you move away from that thought? Can you humbly go within yourself and ask for HELP? Then know and be still that the answer will come to you. ASK. SEEK. TRUST.

2. Set intentions to write. Go deeply inside your soul and be clear about what you want to share with the readers. Prepare your space to write; throw some old things away that no longer serve you...light candles and play soft music in the background.

3. Do you get easily distracted and off-focus? Would you write

better in the library or park away from your home? Are you one who is bothered by noise inside the home and outside? Are you a morning person or a night person? It is okay to turn off your phone for a while so that you can write. Before I start, I enter into a moment of silent meditation to help focus my thoughts. While I am in silence, I see my audience and the angels assisting me. I fix myself a cup of herbal tea, light a candle of incense, and begin to work my plan of action to write.

4. Often in my classes, the question arises as to how to make time for this project. I say, "If writing is important to your soul, then you make the time. Many times, I get up at two or three a.m. to write, as that is when the *Spirit calls to me*, but I go to bed around 6:30 p.m. As I am self-employed, I have more control over when and how often I write than someone with a full-time job away from their home. Go within and ask Spirit for guidance for creating your writing time, and a space to accomplish your goals. I cannot stress this enough in this book: **"set aside time to write."**

5. My inspiration comes from God. Spirit has blessed me with the power necessary to complete each article or chapter in a timely manner. Looking around my space, earth, and home, I find inspiration in the events that happen around me, as well as from my ex-husband, friends, and children. Carrying around a pen and paper with me is first nature; I never know when the urge to write will strike. Some people carry a tape recorder. You may think this is funny, but I often get my best inspiration while running, kickboxing, sleeping, meditating, or in church! Do not let anything discourage you from writing wherever you are; trust your inner guidance.

6. In order to successfully create a book or project, you should formulate a *"plan of action."* Without such a plan, you will never accomplish your goals. For example, I wanted my fourth book to be about what is cooking in your soul. Thus, I put my creativity to work, pulled the cooking concept into stories of my life, and formed the book. Ask God how you can best serve humanity with a book. Then, move forward to create that book.

ce below to create your plan of action. Then, post
can visualize the concept while you are writing your

8. Maybe you want to publish your writings. If so, many c are available to you. You may choose to self-publish. You may s the Internet for self-publishing companies or talk to someone has already published a book in order to gain knowledge. Go t public library or bookstore in order to compare and utilize books how to write and become published. What should you do once yo have written your book and have become self-published? Read the magazine, *Writer's Guide to Publishing.* Resources such as this are exceptionally important when it comes to learning how to find and hire the right agent and sign with the right publishing company. Pray about your writing and ask God to lead you to the right people. Allow yourself to take full ownership of your literary work. Most published authors with major publishing contracts received them with the help of a literary agent. Accept help and support from anyone who you think can offer sound advice. Think inside and outside of the box while writing. Listen to your inner guidance and know your writing craft. Mine is writing "lessons learned" from my life and the lives of others who cross my path. My gift is best used to inspire, instruct, empower, and heal others' lives. My work is categorized as Christian, Spiritual, Biographical, Psychological, Religious, and Non-fiction. My books are sold in all types of religious bookstores and regular ones as well. You must understand what defines your writing in order to market or connect with the right literary agent. I was blessed that Corwin Press called me to develop an educational book on parental involvement. Moreover, the publisher for this book, Westry Wingate Group, has agreed to publish this book! Such instances of luck and blessings do not always happen in the publishing world. Sometimes you have to use persistence to make your own way. Write the book that is deep inside your soul and do not write like another person; write like yourself!

Summary

"Writing is a form of prayer." ~Franz Kafka (1883-1924)

You are a writer and all writing comes from a Universal God in the form of Spirit. As you read my introduction for *In Due Season,* it is my deepest belief that you gained understanding of how to communicate and connect with the reader about the content of your book. Next, start this moment to prepare your heart, soul, and mind to receive information, inspiration, and direction for your book. Use the seven tips given to help jump-start your process and make your plan of action. Do not compare yourself to another writer; step into your own shoes and wear them proudly. What size shoes do you wear? Again, please use your own *key* to open the writing door; it is yours. Do you have the *"inner"* unlock your potential to write books? As you write, remember the written word is a form of prayer.

Meditation for Writers

> **St. Theresa of Lisieux Prayer (1873-1897)**
>
> "May today there be peace within. May you trust that you are exactly where you are meant to be. May you not forget the infinite possibilities that are born of faith in yourself and others. May you use the gifts that you have received, and pass on the love that has been given to you. May you be content with yourself just the way you are. Let this knowledge settle into your bones, and allow your soul the freedom to sing, dance, praise, and love. It is there for each and every one of us."

It is my prayer, my dears, that you find a perfect peace within your soul and know that you are exactly where God would have you to be. Pass your gifts on to others; it will come back to you. So it is.

MY THOUGHTS AND PRAYERS

"Thoughts unspoken are not unknown to the Divine Mind. Desire is prayer; and no loss can occur from trusting God with our desires, that they may be moulded and exalted before they take form in words and in deeds."

~Mary Baker Eddy, founder of Christian Science
(Science and Health with Key to the Scriptures, 1875, p. 1)

Take the time here to write down your thoughts. Remember, they are prayers as well.

Chapter 3
Ready, Set, Go

"The most beautiful thing we can experience is the mysterious."
~Albert Einstein (1879-1955)

As a creative person seeking to start the process of writing a book or project by your own design, until now, *how* do you view yourself? Do you know who you are as a writer? How do you appear at your desk?

____

____

____

____

What do you want to write about? Do you have a clear idea? Novels, Business, Poetry, Fiction, Spirituality, Family History, Cooking, etc....

____

____

____

____

____

Please create an affirmation to use while you write your project and then go to work.

What is your mission for writing your books or projects? Can you be used by Spirit as a channel?

Journal your feelings about writing, right here, right now:

____

____

____

When is your best time to write: early morning, afternoon or night?

____

What do you have to release in order to complete your project?

____

____

____

What is Your Story?

If you are a writer who is lending your expertise to people who read your work, they want to know what makes you an expert in your field. Who are you?

We all have a story to tell. Our stories help others along their paths. Some of you may have been sexually, physically, emotionally, or mentally abused. Your story will enlighten others on their path. Some may have been in a failed marriage, sick, or addicted to drugs. We all have a story to tell that can uplift another and inspire them wherever they might be. In addition, you just may have a creative imagination. What defines you? Before you begin to write, decide who and **what** defines you. Then ask yourself what are the needs of your soul? Do you want to write non-fiction or fiction? Are poems, songs, or paintings the ways by which you desire to express your stories? Do you want to create and market a cookbook? Do you want to provide stories of healing to others who have experienced the same situations that you have experienced in your life? Once you have decided who and what defines you as an author, can you be true to your inner voice and allow it to shine through as you write? Give yourself permission to share your story. Tell **your truth** in your story. Stop being afraid of what your family and friends might say. Be true to the writer within. If you are one to write fiction, wear that hat proudly and expand the concept.

Try this exercise:

In the silence of your desk, office, or the space where you work on your writings, become still and relaxed. Your body is still and your hands too. Soft music is playing in the background. Your feet are folded into the lotus or Indian pose. You will close your eyes, and when you open them you will see the clouds above outside through the trees. Everything outside is still. Words will begin floating into your mind and the Spirit of your own understanding gives you the power to write. You are free to write your truth, your story, as you know it. You will not allow any chains or shackles to hold you down. You have unbound yourself and are free. You will now write. Say, "*I am a writer and Spirit flows to me and through me to write.*" Amen.

Write your story now...

If you need more space, you may want to use a journal or a notebook. Who are you and what makes you an expert on what you want to write? Ask to be a channel for Spirit. Be very clear of your intentions to write your stories.

____

____

How do you feel after writing your story?

The God of your understanding will help you and support your efforts in writing as you make a conscious decision and follow your heart. This is a "spiritual law," cause and effect.

"Do not fear mistakes — there are none." ~**Miles Davis (1926-1991)**

Summary

Everything in creativity starts with nothing and with silence. Then, it is mysteriously made into something. You are a co-creator with the Universal Spirit; you can do whatever you desire. Have clear ideas, use meditation to tap into the Creative Intelligence - the Mind of God, affirm who you are, what you are creating, and why. Know your mission for writing. What do you feel about it? Tell your story boldly; know when the best time is for you to write. Remember to let go of people, places, and things temporarily in order to create a new project. Blessings.

Meditation for Writers

Let us start in a posture of meditation so that the writer within you will come forth right now. Use an incense of meditation from a health food store. Sit in a chair at your desk or on the floor, hands in your lap, and stare at a candle light and think of nothing. Let your mind go blank. Ask for guidance, clarity, communication, and direction from the angels in charge or whoever assists you in your writing. See yourself writing or typing at your personal computer. See the audience you want to speak to. Affirm that you have something to give them when they read the insights contained in your book and learn about your challenges and strengths. Go within and know the truth: that you have something that others can read and grow from on this journey we call earth! Thank your audience for reading your hard work and bless them. Begin the process without fear, doubt, and worry. You can do it. Write your story today; you are a channel to be used by Spirit! So it is!

MY THOUGHTS AND PRAYERS

"Thoughts unspoken are not unknown to the Divine Mind. Desire is prayer; and no loss can occur from trusting God with our desires, that they may be moulded and exalted before they take form in words and in deeds."
~Mary Baker Eddy, founder of Christian Science
(Science and Health with Key to the Scriptures, 1875, p. 1)

Take the time here to write down your thoughts. Remember, they are prayers as well.

CHAPTER 4
COMMITMENT TO YOUR WRITING CRAFT

"God chooses one man with a shout, another with a song, another with a whisper."
~Rabbi Nahman (1928-present)

How did it feel after you wrote a short part of your story? Are you clearer about who you are as a writer? Then, why do we lack commitment and dedication to our craft of writing? God has chosen us to write, to inspire, and to share our talents with others. Yet, we choose not to write and often put it off. **Why?**

____

____

____

Have you ever thought of how to show up as a **writer?** It takes commitment and dedication within your soul to be able to put your pen to paper and let the ideas flow. Many of us are afraid of the word *commitment* relating to anything: relationship, marriage, church, friendship, or vocation. We want to do our best at a craft or vocation; we want to win friendships and gain influence in a relationship; yet, we do not want to do the inner work to establish the commitment to attain success. Often, we act as if what we desire is supposed to come easily for us; in truth, it will come easily and effortlessly if we apply our skills and knowledge to create what we desire. I am writing here about many of us who want to express a gift to write, but hesitate to put our hands to the plow to get the project moving. Our minds are set on writing, yet the heart and soul are over there somewhere in the nothingness and doing nothing. Where is your inner **commitment and dedication to your calling to write?**

Your Uniqueness to the World

How do you feel about your uniqueness to write? Are your feelings about you true, or are they an illusion of what others have shared over the years about your craft of writing? I knew I was going to write a book long before the educational publisher Corwin called me, but I felt inadequate even though I knew inside my soul that I was called by God to write. The Chinese proverb states, "The journey of a thousand miles begins with one step." The feeling that I was called to write was overwhelming, and my job was to eliminate the negative from my mindset. At the same time, I knew Carol S. Batey better than anyone except my Higher Power. In the (NKJ) version of the Bible, 1 Corinthians 1:27, states, "But God has chosen the foolish things of the world to put to shame the wise, and God has chosen the weak things of the world to put to shame the things which are mighty." It is sometimes a challenge to accept our calling and step out on absolute faith in God of the Universe who we have never seen. What is even harder is to take our eyes off our weaknesses and know our worth is not based on what we see in a mirror. We are made in the image and likeness of God, the Higher Mind. Therefore, we can do all things we are to do because we are made just like God and that same God lives within the center of our soul. Can you, my dears, accept who you are and stop the game playing and the wearing of that heavy mask of who you are not?

Following is a portion of the poem "Mask", written by Charles C. Finn (1966):

> "Don't be fooled by me. Don't be fooled by the face I wear for I wear a mask, a thousand masks, masks that I'm afraid to take off, and none of them is me."

Describe in the space below what mask you are taking off in order to commit to your craft of writing.

____

____

____

____

____

The *Encarta Online Dictionary* explains the meaning of *commitment* as follows: "He wasn't ready to commit to the relationship; promise, devotion, entrust." Other words for the word *commitment*, according to the *World Book Complete Word Power Library*, are engagement and dedicate. (p. 206)

I am going to ask you to give yourself permission to fully engage or promise to start to write every day for at least thirty minutes to an hour. If you find it difficult to agree to this, then I ask you to remove the mask from whatever it is in your soul that makes you fearful:

____

____

____

____

____

A COMMITMENT AND DEDICATION PROMISE

I, ____, promise that I will write at least one hour per day. I will not judge the content of what pours out of my soul from pen to paper. I will write without the use of a personal computer. In addition, I will accept my work as it is given unto me from Spirit. I will write starting today. I say, "YES!" No longer will I compare myself with others; I will own what is mine. I accept me! I accept me! I have been my biggest critic; I am no longer under those bondages. I look no longer for outside validation; I look within my own soul I am led by the Holy Spirit. Amen.

"But the anointing which you have received from Him abides in you, and you do not need that anyone teach you; but as the same anointing teaches you concerning all things, and is true, and is not a lie, and just as it has taught you, you will abide in Him."

~1 John 2:27 (KJV)

Summary

Let us make a commitment and a dedication to understand that Destiny is calling our souls to write. Do you hear the voice within calling you? I do, and I know you do too. Maybe there is a knock from Spirit on the heart, mind, and soul of your body. Answer the call, my dears, you can do it. Believe in yourself and show up as a writer. Making a commitment is a scary feeling for many folks. It can be a sacred bond that is sealed by a promise to action to do something like WRITE! You are a unique expression of the Divine; this is who you are, not the illusions told to you by others and your lower self. Take time to listen to your higher self. Tune into your higher power and let the negative thoughts of who you *think* you are float away into nothingness. Release those masks; they are just too heavy. Let them go; be the real you and step into your desired destiny to write.

Meditation for Writers

As you look within your soul with your inner eyes, see your desires for writing. The desires are knowledge, wisdom, understanding of who you are, insights into what you are hearing from Spirit, and the ability to tap into your inner soul's power. As you prayerfully come into the knowledge of what to put on paper, give thanks to God. With that action, more things will be revealed to you. Thank you, God. Amen.

MY THOUGHTS AND PRAYERS

"Thoughts unspoken are not unknown to the Divine Mind. Desire is prayer; and no loss can occur from trusting God with our desires, that they may be moulded and exalted before they take form in words and in deeds."

~Mary Baker Eddy, founder of Christian Science
(Science and Health with Key to the Scriptures, 1875, p. 1)

Take the time here to write down your thoughts. Remember, they are prayers as well.

Chapter 5
Be Still And Know That I AM God

"There in the silences it speaks louder than words." ~Anonymous

As I sit this day in church, listening to the Unity message, the words *"Be still and know that I AM God"* (Psalm 46:10 KJV) are written above the platform. While listening to the minister's message, I saw again, *Be Still,* and a childlike wonder came over me to ask myself, "Carol, why can't we **be still to write and to hear from the God-Power within**?" Seeking additional insights, I looked to *The World Book Complete Word Power Library* (1981), and discovered another word for *be* is "rest". (p. 180) Within the same book, other words for *Still* are "calm, silent, hushed, peaceful, and noiseless". (p. 394) Do you get the big picture yet? My dears, when the mind is quiet, peaceful and still, the inspiration from our Higher Power flows or comes unto us for our own personal insights or to share with another. We are often too busy doing this or that, moving and going. The Birthing of our Writing dreams will come to us in the quiet meditative state when our minds are still from the day. What usually happens to me is when I am not consciously seeking an idea or words, they flow into my mind and my heart connects with the information being channeled through me. A still, small voice is what I have heard in the past or just a strong feeling to pay close attention and block out the noises that surround me, as well as tune out what I see. Can you learn to become still and disciplined enough to be a channel for good to flow through your mind and body? YES or NO?

How to Learn to BE STILL?

Have you ever heard of a "Spiritual Practice?" In my third book, *Poise for the Runway of Your Life* (2009 p. 250), I write about the concept.

Marilyn Ferguson states, *"The spiritual quest begins, for most people, as a search for meaning."* Stillness is a spiritual discipline taught in the martial arts, some religions, yoga, prayer, and meditation. To achieve stillness, you are first taught to center yourself by looking within. To accomplish this, you must let go of your conscious thoughts, empty your mind of all thoughts, and turn your focus inward to your heart center. How does that feel to you? Practice centering your thoughts and yourself when you are anxious or distracted from your runway or writings. Go to a place where interruptions and distractions can be kept to a minimum. Stop, breathe, and focus inwardly toward the center of your heart. Envision the wind is blowing with God's presence. Peace and calmness will begin to occur. As the centering starts, you will start the process of being in tune with the God-Power within your soul. It will take practice and dedication to learn and to continue to tap into your Higher Power – the **God** within your soul.

Saint Teresa of Avila, Our Teacher

Do you **know** GOD? Another part of the scripture in Psalms is *"and know that I am GOD."* St. Teresa of Avila, born in Spain in 1515, will help you, the reader, to **know** GOD. She was a devoted Catholic nun, mystic, and author whose teachings instruct, inspire, delight our souls' path, and illuminate our personal runways. After she calmed her rebellious stage and knew God, she accepted God's love and Grace, and He became her Beloved at an early age. With no formal education, she reached heights and public recognition beyond anyone's expectations, mostly hers. Her accomplishments were all done with great humility. Scholars recognized her deep spiritual wisdom and dedication to her Beloved. She was never taught by "learned men." She answered God's call to become a mystic. Her wisdom and holy talents were a gift from God. Following her "spiritual practice," she devoted herself to humble prayer and meditation daily, sometimes all day long. Despite her spiritual practice being in place, she never felt worthy to embrace the presence of God's grace. Yet, this woman of no formal education won favor with scholars. Today, we would say she lacked self-esteem. Although she is now considered a saint, she had a mind and body full of doubts, fears, illness, and in her own words, dullness (depression). This remarkable woman prayed day and night. She relied solely upon

God and herself for her spiritual education. She came to know God. How well do you KNOW God, the God of your understanding?

____

____

____

Prayer and Meditation: The First KEY

Prayer and *meditation* were Saint Teresa's first **key** to her spiritual practice nearly 600 years ago. Along with *prayer* and *meditation,* she practiced humility; this was her entry and it could be yours too: the *key* that opened the Door to the DIVINE. She released her personal self daily *to know God.* How often do you practice those first two elements of the first *key: prayer* and *meditation?*

____

____

____

We are often ruled by our ego, pride, and false humility. Releasing our personal self to God daily can be a positive spiritual practice we adopt. Since the era of St. Teresa of Avila, we have learned that positive self-esteem, dignity, and faith in one's self will reinforce our direction and focus. This spiritual practice can be accomplished humbly in the presence of God as we enter into prayer in Silence, in "the place of the Most High."

Saint Teresa had many visions while meditating. These visions created books. During one instance, she saw a diamond with many shapes and facets. It was a castle with many chambers, which she likened to the soul. This castle had seven rooms; each one had a key to the center room. We are only going to learn about two rooms and their keys. If you would like to follow up on the additional keys, I recommend you to roam her book, *Interior Castle*. According to Saint Teresa, the chief area of the seven rooms is in the center of the castle. This is where Spirit resides and where the most secret things pass between God and the soul. In her book, *Interior Castle*, she shares how the first room in the castle is prayer and meditation. In *The Book of My Life,* she affirms that the Beloved bestows a sweet blessing upon those who persevere in prayer:

> "Prayer is the doorway to the kind of exquisite gifts he has given me. If we keep that door closed, how can he give us what we need? The "Beloved" may be waiting to grace our soul with delight, but he cannot get in! Unless he finds the soul solitary, empty, and longing for his love, there is nothing he can do." (p. 55)

We place challenges of darkness in our way, we do nothing to remove them, and then want God to assist us! How badly do you want to write your books? Remove your obstacles and then seek the exquisite gifts that are yours.

"The endurance of darkness is preparation for great light."
~Saint John of the Cross (1542-1591)

A Spiritual Practice: The Second KEY

The teacher St. Teresa tells us that a *spiritual practice* must be in place before the soul can advance to the second room. We are not going to talk about all of the rooms here in this book, just the **two rooms**. I would admonish you to read her books and educate yourself on what she taught. She asserts that her spiritual practice consists of **prayer, meditation, listening to sermons, edifying conversations, good company, and reading uplifting books.** These tools increased her powers, and the power of her students to resist temptation and to focus on their missions for their God. Once we seek deeper spiritual practice and paths, we are often confronted with opposition, distractions, or challenges. St. Teresa informs us that our power to resist temptations increases when we know that we have the tools to combat them. Your spiritual practice is your insurance for the runway of your life.

What is your insurance for the runway of your life?

"Stop the words now. Open the window in the center of your chest, and let the spirits fly in and out."
~Rumi (1207-1273)

Carol Batey's Spiritual Practice

Seven years ago, I developed my own spiritual practices of attending a Center for Spiritual Worship, entering into the Silence, eating wholesome foods, fasting often, exercising, prayer, meditation, reading, listening to enjoyable and uplifting music and TV programs, journaling, and tapping into my emotional support system of friends.

Claim your peace, inspiration, and develop a spiritual practice for yourself and implement it today.

"Learn to be calm and you will always be happy."
~Paramhansa Yogananda (1893-1952)

Summary

You ask, "Carol, what does "being still and knowing that I Am God" have to do with writing?" My dears, everything. Creation starts in the silence of our hearts and minds. We must have a childlike wonder within our souls and not be full of pride, ego, and the attributes of the lower-self. As we seek the Higher-Self, we become peaceful and calm. We must learn to go within to seek the knowledge and wisdom given to us by our Higher Power to write. In the act of becoming disciplined to a *spiritual practice,* the words will flow into our heads, to the hand, then to the paper. Learn from St. Teresa. She is there to teach us; she had no formal education, yet, went on to earn praise from her Bishops and the community. Her books, *Interior Castle* and *My Book of My Life* are in most public libraries. What are you waiting for? Do it today!

Meditation for Writers

If you are one who desires to write to inspire others, I leave you with St. Teresa of Avila's words for you to meditate upon. Know that God wants to use you as a channel to write.

Christ Has No Body Now But YOURS

"Christ has no body now but yours,

No hands, no feet on earth but yours,

Yours are the eyes with which he looks

Compassion on this world,

Yours are the feet with which he walks to do good,

Yours are the hands, with which he blesses all the world.

Yours are the hands,

Yours are the feet,

Yours are the eyes,

You are his body.

Christ has no body now on earth but yours."

~Saint Teresa of Avila

In the Silence

"In the silence there is peace. In the silence there is unspoken Joy. In the silence there's release from a world full of chaos and noise. So, I wait for these precious moments. When I hear all that could never be said. And right here in this Holy Silence. I find God, I find myself."

~Jack Fowler
www.jackfowler.info

My Thoughts And Prayers

"Thoughts unspoken are not unknown to the Divine Mind. Desire is prayer; and no loss can occur from trusting God with our desires, that they may be moulded and exalted before they take form in words and in deeds."

~Mary Baker Eddy, founder of Christian Science
(Science and Health with Key to the Scriptures, 1875, p. 1)

Take the time here to write down your thoughts. Remember, they are prayers as well.

Chapter 6
Awakening And Attracting Prosperity Using Your God-Mind

"Prosperity is a worthy goal of aspiration
and a promised reward for good living."
~Abraham Joshua Heschel (1907-1972)

When I was creating my destiny to become a model and writer at age 51, I moved from the security of my hometown and apartment. I left for a place unknown to me, a little country town outside of Atlanta, Georgia called Carrollton. Wow, all I can say is that I said "Yes" to God and had no idea what was being unfolded for me until *I stepped into the destiny*. I tell this story at length in my other books, but for my purposes here, I just want you to know that when I arrived, my rent, water, and electricity were taken care of for nine months in exchange for me taking care of the property. At the time, most of my income was from my profession as a massage therapist. I left my clients in Nashville to pursue my childhood dreams and live my destiny. Therefore, I had to recreate my life with a blind faith and trust in the Universal Mind. When I was twelve, I wanted to model and write books. Once I hit age 49, I suddenly remembered my inner vision and dreams of my youth and began using them to create a new me.

Live and Create Your Destiny

We have talked about commitment and being still to know what God would have you to write. After a few months in Carrollton, God gave me a positive statement to say once every morning, a *metaphysical affirmation applied with faith*. This was the start of shaping and forming my *mental attitude* to attract to me what I needed to write, teach, coach, live, read, and to function in the country setting, which was all new for me. The word *metaphysics*, as defined in *The Ernest Holmes New Thought Dictionary,* is "viewing the universe as a mental and spiritual system, governed by laws of thought. Man, being part of this system, discovers the same laws inherent within his own being and may apply them to definite purpose". (Holmes, 1991, p.93) The phrase *New Thought Movement,* according to Holmes in the same book, is "the group's societies, religious and spiritual organizations built upon the *New Thought* philosophy, leaving room for ample independent individualism. The principles governing the *New Thought Movement* are universal, but individually and independently applied". *(p. 100)*

Have you ever embarked on a new path and the path was unknown unto you? How did you feel?

____

____

____

____

Metaphysical Affirmation

This is what I was given and now I ask that you use it too: "I have prosperity, abundance, happiness, success, and health in my life, world and affairs." So it is! When saying, "So it is" the affirmation is sealed; it is a statement of truth. This affirmation also programs your subconscious to transfer this information to the consciousness of your mind. In turn, this forms a mental attitude for attracting what you desire!

To me, metaphysics is the use of your mind to co-create with your Higher Power, to form what you desire to manifest in your world. This can be coupled with ancient teachings from many masters, guides, and sages, who have walked this planet.

The teachings of metaphysics are psychology mixed with philosophy and a mystical approach.

Let us Stop and Define the Affirmation

What is *prosperity* to you? Is it riches of money, houses, land, cars, designer clothing, and glory to be seen by men and women? **It is a state of mind**. What is your mind feeling right now?

____

____

____

____

____

____

____

____

How do you view the word *abundance*? The average person hears the word abundance and thinks of lavish riches, extravagances, etc. In a spiritual sense, the word means *receiving from an overflow of the bounties of the universe*. Often, we want to think only in terms of lack and limitation; however, this is far from the truth of who we are as spiritual beings. We are richly blessed from our association with the Universal Mind of God. There is only one Mind in this big Universe and that is the Mind of God. All that God has is ours, so claim your entitlement by repeating this metaphysical affirmation often.

Happiness is the next word in the metaphysical affirmation. I know you have heard this stated by many, "Happiness is an inside job." Let us observe: what is an inside job? Stop right here and say this three times to your inner-self with eyes closed: "I am happy!" Breathe; again say, "I am happy!" Again, breathe; release and let out "I am happy!" As your feet are on the ground or the floor and your hands on your lap, what did you feel? This can also be called self or auto-suggestion.

Wikipedia online *Encyclopedia* describes *happiness* this way: "state of mind of feeling characterized by contentment, love, satisfaction, pleasure, or joy." Philosophers and religious thinkers often define happiness in terms of living a good life, or flourishing rather than an emotion." Do you get the big picture?

What does *success* mean to you? I would like to recommend that you read *The Prosperity Bible* by Napoleon Hill, et al. (2007) This book contains historical accounts of a number of individuals who became successful using the world's greatest secrets to achieving wealth and prosperity. In addition, I would like to suggest that you read *Think and Grow Rich* by Napoleon Hill (1937), as it contains the secrets of how to become successful in your life in spite of your social and economic standing. Mr. Hill says, "*Success comes to those who become success conscious. And failure comes to those who indifferently allow themselves to become failure conscious.*" The object of these two books I have suggested for you to read is to help you learn how to change your inner thoughts from failing to successful thinking. Affirm: "*I am successful, there are no limitations holding me back, just my own mind-set.*" And it is so!

"Health," it has been said, "is not a commodity to be bargained for. Instead, it has to be earned." Can you take a personal responsibility for your well-being? Many master teachers and spiritual healers have taught that sickness starts in the mind and works its way into our bodies. Once you declare or affirm that you are healthy, your mind tells your body and soul that you are healthy. Can you say my body knows no sickness? By integrating a spiritual practice and preventative health measures, you can protect your body and soul from sickness. "*Let your food be your medicine and medicine be your food,*" Hippocrates said.

Creating Your Day

Maybe you want to create your own metaphysical affirmation for creating your day. Take the time now and do so.

____

____

____

____

____

____

____

____

____

____

____

____

And so it is!

What does this chapter have to do with writing?

It is my desire for you to be a successful entrepreneur writer. With that, I want to make sure that you draw and attract everything you desire for your writing craft. In previous chapters, I have asked you to develop a *spiritual practice*. Have you? This concept will help your mind, body, soul, and spirit to relax, hear, and feel from the Universal Mind. The process will start the awakening to your inner journey to write! As you attune your subconscious mind first to follow the conscious mind through meditation and your affirmation, your mind becomes still and clear. Then, you will become open to ideas, thoughts, and inspirations to put to paper for a book or project. The Universal Mind of God wants to flow through our bodies as a channel for good to help inspire others along their paths. You must start with a surrender of your ego or lower self in order to achieve and create your writing craft. Learning to trust and use your intuition is scary at first, but do not give in to fears that block your divine destiny to write. To be a successful writer, you must not lean just on *intellect* alone, but also your spiritual side.

Living in Carrollton, GA

After a few months of living in that unusual country setting, I surrendered to my path for that time being. Destiny had called me there for a reason that was unknown. I actually thought that I was called because I received a major modeling contract at age 51. That was just a seed that pulled me into that *sacred place*. In this *sacred place*, I had to release and let go of what I thought I knew about my journey's false beliefs and tune in daily to my Sacred Source. As I let go I said, "Yes" again to God and developed my third book, *Poise for the Runway of Your Life* (2007), which is about the journey of traveling on your perspective runway (pathways) of your life. There, I was able to visit the public library daily and order the spiritual books needed to assist and enlighten me on the journey. Next, as I set important time aside to write and research material, I felt the presence of unseen teachers and guides, and a strong presence of the Holy Spirit of the Universal Mind. Many times as I traveled to and from the library, books would almost speak to me saying, "Take me home," and I did. Therefore, being awakened to get out of bed at two a.m. to study, I found inspiring information to deepen my own journey that I was able to communicate with my readers! My thoughts had to be attuned daily to the goodness of the Universal Mind. As I am writing this handbook to you now, it is three a.m. I currently live five minutes away from the Nashville airport. During the day, the airplanes often fly so low that I can barely focus, but at this time in the early morning, the sky is quiet!

However, I am not a perfect being living on this earth, as I get into situations where I face and experience negative thinking. Haven't you experienced that too? You recognize that your mind has been filled with depression, a negative pattern. You cut it out of your consciousness first by recognizing it and then filling your mind with positive thoughts and thankfulness until you start to *believe it!*

My dears, you attract what you believe. What do you believe about your inner dreams to write? Be honest.

___

___

___

___

___

___

___

Do You Let Others Get in Your Way?

I no longer listen to outside voices who do not know my deepest desires and calling, but I have in the past. Only the voice within my own soul and the Universal God is what I choose to listen to. Now, there are times when God sends a true messenger; I then ponder their insights and move forward to implement what they have shared. Be open and respectful to those voices to listen and then to act.

Summary

Can you move from a place of unknown and step into your destiny? So often, it is not clear what that place is or where. This is when you surrender and say, "YES" to the movement inside your soul. It takes blind faith and trust in the Universal Mind. What were your dreams when you were small? Please create a metaphysical affirmation and use it daily. Here is a review from my chapter on affirmation: Prosperity is a state of mind; Abundance is an overflow from the universe; Happiness, as you know now, is an inside job; Success comes to those who "think" they are successful; Health is having a well-being of no disease in the physical, mental, and social body. Say, "I have prosperity, abundance, and happiness, and success, health in my life, world, and affairs." So be it.

Meditation for Writers

Think positively about your ability to attract your desires for creating an entrepreneur writing business. Now, close your eyes, turn off your mind, and drift off into the blue and white clouds of expectations. Destiny is calling your soul to write, open the windows of your soul to receive the words, and draw the words into your soul's consciousness. Take some cleansing breaths and release fear, doubt and worry of what you felt you could not do. Breathe in success, abundance, prosperity, health, and happiness; it is yours. With a Divine appointment, it is your season to flourish. Say, "*I am a successful entrepreneur writer.*" So it is!

My Thoughts And Prayers

"Thoughts unspoken are not unknown to the Divine Mind. Desire is prayer; and no loss can occur from trusting God with our desires, that they may be moulded and exalted before they take form in words and in deeds."

~Mary Baker Eddy, founder of Christian Science
(Science and Health with Key to the Scriptures, 1875, p. 1)

Take the time here to write down your thoughts. Remember, they are prayers as well.

Chapter 7
The Right Time Is Now

"The essence of writing is to know your subject."
~David McCullough (1993)

In Chapter 2, I showed you how I connect and communicate with my readers. How well do you know your subject and story lines? It does not matter how great you are with the written word, as a writer, one must speak to the reader's interest and pain. There must be a connection and a value to what you are communicating. The reader wants to know that your story lines will impact their soul and give him or her a solution. Can you visually see your target audience, the age, how much money they make, children or none, type of spirituality or none, where they live in the world, ethnic background? Be very clear whom you are targeting.

Your target audience will want to know how your book will benefit them once they make the monetary investment. Let us take time to think about this statement. Write your thoughts here:

____

____

____

____

____

____

Target audiences will enter a bookstore with questions in mind. They will seek research on the web of how your book will solve their internal conflicts, solutions, or challenges. Think about this and then write your thoughts here:

____

____

____

____

____

____

What Kind of Writer Are You?

Are you one who desires to create a "self-help or inspirational book?" Can you write to yourself? Maybe you have been in the same situation, and neither a book nor a person was available to you. What did you do? Can you remember? Did you keep a journal as you were led by Spirit to write your path down? Did you use your intuition as an act to sense knowledge that was impressed into your mind? Perhaps you were helped by another person. Can you list that information and site them? Are you true with your feelings of what you went through, or have you suppressed the events? Yet, somehow, do you still seem to think you are not on top of your challenges? If this is so, then you may need to write in a soul journal for a while until you are honest with your inner feelings about what happened. Can you take personal responsibility of the challenges of your life, world, and affairs? You cannot write to help others, and play the blame and shame game, too. However, one must take full ownership of their part of what happened. Nonetheless, they must understand what is theirs and then move on. This life we live is a school where we come to learn lessons and to grow spiritually. For those of us who write "*life lessons*" from our lives, this is our call. We must look at the glass as very full of lessons, wisdom, spiritual knowledge and insights. On the other hand, people who experience tragedy, job or income loss, abuse, challenges in health, sadness from death, grief, etc., pass the blame onto others. Conversely, these people look at the glass very empty with nothing inside. Then again, if the person learns the lessons, forgive others, themselves, and their Higher Power (if they have one), they become complete, whole, and perfect to carry the inspirational message of love, forgiveness, hope and the *lessons learned* to others on the planet.

My Call

All throughout my life, I have faced and experienced obstacles, adversity of sexual abuse, emotional abuse, and other negative emotions that I took on, but have released by forgiving and expressing compassion to others at the same time. At this time, I am 56 years young with many *life lessons* to share. As a child, I knew and sensed my destiny was different from my peers. I just did not know how different my destiny was until I started to write my stories without fear and share them with the world. My plan is have a sustainable writing, coaching and speaking business and live in prosperity and abundance.

Friedrich Nietzsche (1844-1900) states: "Our destiny commands us even when we do not yet know what it is; it is the future which guides the rule to the present."

I have had many people ask me how I can write about my family, children and my ex-husband. They continue to ask, "How can you tell the truth" about the sexual and the emotional abuse suffered? "How can I not," I answer, if I am totally at peace about the situation and my ownership of what happened. I see the glass very full, not empty. Mysteries finally answered, and healing occurs for all those who are open to be healed. Everyone involved in tough situations wants inner healing. They are perfectly comfortable with their station in life, shifting the blame and still shaming others. Yet, they are all alone hiding behind many masks because they are too afraid to see the blessings of the glass being full. Often, the person writing about those challenges of life must set the intentions of why they are writing.

Why Are You Writing?

Do you want to write to harm another? Why are you writing? Ask your inner guidance, and then do some soul searching to understand why Spirit has chosen you to bring this book forth. Will it help assist another on their dark path? Can it illuminate another soul's journey to free them from the stronghold of bondage, of fear, of hate, of blame and shame? Many who have faced abuse from another, turned, and abused others feel they are not good enough to share their stories or be healed within. Numerous believe that the God out there is extremely mad at them. They think they are nothing in comparing themselves to others. Scores of people who have challenges in life think others are more important, and no one can really relate to their story. Therefore, "I must keep my story to myself; what do I have to share"?

This is the right time for you to ponder, "Why do you want to write?"

____

____

____

____

____

____

____

____

Have you done your inner forgiveness work?

____

____

____

____

Can you honestly write about what happened to you in the past? Then, can you identify the lessons and move on to help others?

____

____

____

____

If more time and space is needed, please write in a notebook or journal ...

I can write about my children's hurts, drug usage, emotional upsets, negative behaviors, as well as their victories because I ask for their permission. My focus is from a mother, a parent's viewpoint, to assist other parents in similar situations. Writing about lessons learned from my marriage was easy once I took full responsibility for my part as a wife. Then, I applied forgiveness toward my ex-husband and myself. He never wanted me to work outside of the home. Upon meeting him, I had just finished a Fashion and Merchandising degree. After we said, "I do", he said he did not want me to work. At that juncture, I thought my dreams of modeling and writing books were gone with the wind. After twenty-one years of marriage, I filed for divorce at age forty-one. After the divorce and the stress of the children, I gained forty-three pounds. At that point, I took personal responsibility for my inner healing and weight loss. I attended massage school first; then later at forty-nine, I woke up and remembered my inner dreams, my destiny.

I went to modeling school at fifty with the intent of getting a modeling contract outside of Nashville. Most of the details of this experience are in my second book, *In Due Season: Destiny is Calling Your Soul.* In my third book, *Poise for the Runway of Your Soul,* the stories written in one chapter are about my son's drug use from ages 12-20 years old and about the abuse I suffered. My fourth book, *What's Cooking in Your Soul,* shares lessons learned from my marriage, how to move forward, all of my six children's challenges and victories, my sexual abuse, and forgiveness. This is my story. Now it is the right time to tell yours.

Summary

What are your life lessons from your past? Do you even know? This is the right time to examine your reasons to write your books. Your future guides the present, and with clear intentions set of why you are called to write your stories, you gain inner peace. Why are you writing? Ask yourself; DOES THIS MAKE SENSE? Connect with your reader on a soul level, know your target audience and speak to their pain and interest within their soul.

Meditation for Writers

This is your time to write this day, this hour, this week, this month. You are a creative being who has been called to develop books for others. You can do it. See your past, list the “life lessons”, and share those inner gifts with your reader. Do not neglect this gift, stir it up! So be it!

My Thoughts And Prayers

"Thoughts unspoken are not unknown to the Divine Mind. Desire is prayer; and no loss can occur from trusting God with our desires, that they may be moulded and exalted before they take form in words and in deeds."

~Mary Baker Eddy, founder of Christian Science
(Science and Health with Key to the Scriptures, 1875, p. 1)

Take the time here to write down your thoughts. Remember, they are prayers as well.

Chapter 8
Your Project Is Finished, Now What?

"He who does not look ahead, remains behind." - Spanish Proverb

Your book or project is almost finished, or published; the CD or DVD is completed, your ministry or volunteer work has started, the schooling for your new trade and mission is done, your project is over and accomplished. What is the next move of your new journey to "get the message" out? What are your true feelings about starting your own publishing company, using a self-publisher to put your book on demand, self-promotions, branding, career building, the revolution of social media (Facebook, etc.), direct services, podcasting, online media, viral marketing, making a book or project trailer, e-book promotions, blog, publicity, e-mail newsletters and articles, webinar, marketing, and promotion**?** Are your thoughts based on limiting fear-based beliefs about your circumstances, such as the way you were raised, lack of skills and talent, money, or the way you think or look? None of that is important for "getting your message" out to the media and public. Oh, and do not let me forget that you do not know how to use a personal computer or social networking. So, you think you have a lack of education and no so-called opportunities. As you have read my story and the stories about others who write, you can see that you can be successful at marketing your project – and yourself. You can become a prosperous entrepreneur and successful writer. You can have a sustainable business in whatever medium you chose, but you must work at it.

Understanding a Few Terms

Do you understand the meaning of social media, the latest power of marketing on the Internet? Social media is used to network with others. You can make friends with all types of people from all over the world, and reconnect with those you have missed over the years. On Facebook alone, there are over 200 million users and fans, and as of the date of this publication, they are the number one social media network. It is the new way people communicate and creates a new platform for networking.

If you are marketing your project or book, you must still know your audience and sell to them. You can link your website and blog (a written story about something someone wants to share with the world). One great feature about social networking is that you can link your site with another. Many become a leader and push their causes to participants. For example, I send out invites for my workshops to everyone because I also do a webinar via the web. If you find you are too busy or a person who does not like to participate in social networking, but realizes its' importance, there are other services like *Hootsuite.com* that can assist you. I personally employ a virtual assistant who handles my social media. A virtual assistant is similar to an administrative assistant, only he or she works virtually (via online) from their home or offsite from their employer. All of my editors and assistants are located in other states, which I have found on *Hiremymom.com*.

Webinars are also called web conferencing. It enables the user to conduct training, workshops, and live meetings from his or her own computer, and is connected to other participants via the Internet. My first webinar was just last summer, where I incorporated a PowerPoint presentation. I used WebEx for my host, but there are many others. Often, you are permitted a free trial period on many of these types of websites.

Internet Podcasting is becoming increasingly popular. A podcast is an audio file that can be delivered to many people via a Really Simple Syndication (RSS) feed. The RSS feed automatically sends a file or link to someone who subscribes to it. Every three months, I place an e-newsletter or article on certain sites that are free, as well as on my own website. An e-newsletter can also be used to advertise your goods and services; no paper is required unless you want to pass your information out, such as a flyer. Another option is to offer a percentage off on your e-newsletter and e-books.

Align Yourself with a Higher Power

First, you must align yourself with your Higher Power for a spiritual and personal transformation to accomplish what is needed to "get your message" out. Please, start right now, taking personal responsibility for your mental attitude and your inner thoughts. Unless you are inspiring and helping another, you need to stop nursing and rehearsing your seemly past failures and abuses. Break yourself free from holding on to that negative and useless energy that caused frustration and a robbing of creative energy. Learn the lesson from your past experiences, but do not be bound by them. Learn the "life lessons" and failure comes to those who indifferently allow themselves to become failure conscious. " *Look ahead*, as the Spanish proverb goes, *you don't want to remain behind.* "

Affirm right now:

I am no longer bound and shackled to my past story lines, but free to create my future as a new creation.

Questions for You:

- Do you have a strong belief in yourself and your product?
- Can you see the positive in others and not in you?
- Can you seize the moment and take opportunities?
- Are you a giver, or are you a taker?
- Can you reach out to others in a form of social media such as Twitter or Facebook, etc.?
- Where does your attention and time go: on the solution or the problem?
- To become successful, one must not give up, but practice persistence and determination. Can you do this?
- Do you step up to the plate and take full responsibility for your actions? No blaming or shaming others?

Tapping into Your Resources

John C Maxwell has said, *"Success landmarks are internal, not external. Look for landmarks."* How often do we look for success on our outside? We do not even think to look internally; that is the last place we look. Instead, we look to others – who they are and what they are driving, clothes they are wearing, etc. Then, we look to see what our peers are doing, saying, and wearing. We never stop to think how we feel about moving up the ladder. We, as humans, just want to keep up with the Joneses. Look within your soul, not outside yourself. How do you feel about moving into your own success?

Association with successful, positive business-minded people will help you increase your knowledge and promote yourself better. If you are not involved in an organization or a meet-up group that could help advances your business, then this is the time for you to seek one. Try joining an organization, meet-up group, club, business-networking group, business chamber in your city, mixer's for your niche. Try using Internet groups or classes, social media venue, or Internet marketing venue that will shed insights on getting your message perfected and out to the public. A few authors are hiring business, writing, and speaking coaches. They may be found via a search on the Internet or in the yellow pages. Ask successful entrepreneur writers for advice on an internet chat or on any of the social media. If you are one who wants to learn how to improve your speaking, you may want to join Toastmasters. If you want to step up to another level and build a speaking business, join a local chapter of National Speaker Association or other speaking associations. The NSA helps give you insights and information to build your speaking business.

Update Your Marketing Skills

Today's marketing plans are not what they used to be. You may want to take classes in marketing and/or learn how to surf, blog, do a podcast in an Internet class. The Internet is the new and fast way of marketing any products directly to the consumers. Videos are also a new marketing tool on the web; they inform and tell stories. You need to keep them short, less than ten minutes.

Press releases used to be the way to reach certain people in the media. Today, the Internet, as well as social media such as Twitter and Facebook reaches not only the media but also a mass global market of readers and more if you are a writer. Having interaction with the news media is still important. I follow my local hometown newspaper and utilize their expertise to get my message out. In December 2010, I was in *Ebony* magazine. The writer initially sent me an email and asked if I would be an expert for her column. I, of course, said, "yes!' She mentioned she had already visited my website. When I asked how she was able to find me, she said she did research on me via the web. You get the idea now? A person who wants to be successful and known in their work must build an Internet presence of their works and their brand. Your business as a writer must implement key words and phrases, so when someone is surfing or searching the web, it can be found. For example, my key words are spiritual and personal transformation. What is your brand? As a person in the writing business, wanting to sell books and get speaking engagements booked, the Internet is your target to the masses. The aspiring author's goal is to win business. You do this with great content to the target readers.

Do you understand the concept of e-books? According to Author House's self-publishing newsletter, there were 441.3 million e-books sold in the world in 2010! All of my books are e-books that can be read on a portable, fast reader called a Nook (Barnes and Noble), or a Kindle (Amazon). This is the new landscape of publishing called epublishing. Some Smartphones and Smashwords can download books as well. I receive more of the royalties this way than through the books that are printed. Many authors offer an e-book for free on their personal website, which is such a great marketing and promotion tool.

Don't ever admit that the world has not given you an opportunity." -
Napoleon Hill

Marketing and Promotions: What Are They?

My dears, do you know the difference between *marketing* and *promotions?* Are they both the same? No, but they go hand in hand. Are you the service? I developed my services for my books; I am the service. Is there a product that you have developed that is a service or project? On the other, I create books and my books are my products. The online *Encarta Dictionary* describes *marketing* as "The business activity of presenting products or services in such a way as to make them desirable." As I searched Wikipedia, I learned also that *marketing* is "an action of set intentions for creating, delivering, communicating, and selling your products that create customer value." This may also be used for maintaining a satisfying partnership between you and your customers or clients. *Promotions,* as defined on Wikipedia, "help get your message, word, and product out by offering discounts, coupons, or free merchandise to the customers." Stop and think about these two terms and write here what you understand about them:

Marketing:

____

____

____

____

____

____

____

Promotions:

____

____

____

____

____

____

____

How To Do It?

Boy, it is so easy to find the creative time to implement our dreams and bring them to pass. After the dream has been created, the challenge is how to market the product and sell it to the public and businesses. Time and time again, we do not attempt to **market or promote and the project stays on the shelf, in the drawer, in the home, or in the business.** Most of us start from the ground floor and work our way up. We become the inventor, creator, the advertiser, the shipper, the manager, the deliverer, and the candlestick maker. That is a big job, but it is your product, your invention and your creation, not someone else's. We are everything.

Take a pause, breathe deeply. Take a healthy dose of fresh air into your lungs slowly. Now, breathe it all out. What you just read may be overwhelming. Affirm: **I can do this next stop on my journey. With the Spirit living inside of me and assisting me, I will.** Right now at this moment, if you have a project finished or you would like to wrap it up, make a commitment to do so. Apply faith in your Higher Power and yourself that you will bring your dreams and product to pass and make it a reality. Marketing and promotion are the two most important steps after bringing your project to a close. Are you ready? Hear how I market and promote my books and signature workshops:

My First Book

As you know, this is my fifth book in 15 years. With my first book, I had the contract through Corwin Press Educational Publisher before the content of the book was determined. I still had to create and write the publisher a book proposal and send it to them. Long before that book came into reality, I saw the vision of why the book was needed and who should read it. Then, I stopped there and envisioned educators, administrators, parent-leaders, and community leaders that needed the information presented within this book that was still in my mind. Within that proposal, I also had to submit a marketing plan for the book:

The Why

This book is needed to guide those who are working with parents to help utilize their talents within the schools. This will enhance their child's learning.

The Who

I wrote down the vision of my new book and how to market it. Who was my target? What was my target demographic and age? How was I going to get this information about my new book to the "target demographic"?

The What

The vision of who, what, how, why and when is important. The plan to action was then to go out in Nashville (where I lived) and across the United States to as many educational conferences and workshops as possible to get business cards and network with others. Remember, I did not know how to work a computer nor did I have one to use for all my research. This was 1994. My marketing plan for one of my books is at the back of this book.

The How

Networking and believing in your dreams, as many of you already know, is the key. Most people just want to rely on the Internet alone, but a personal contact by phone and regular mail is very important. Do not underestimate the value of personal contact, face to face; though it appears to be a lost art now. As time went by while I was writing, I collected business cards and kept the inner vision of me sending out a letter, a flyer, a one-sheet informing those new contacts about the book once it went to press. This was my marketing plan in 1995 which I started long before the book came out. Corwin Press sent my free, one-sheet about my book, and I sent out 400 by mail, utilizing no Internet. As of today, I still use regular mail. A one-sheet is all the information about the product on one sheet. It has the ISBN #'s, copyright, release date, a picture of the book or product, and information about the book. There is a sample in the resources section in the back of this book.

The When

Most people stop after the first year. I still mail out flyers about my first book as well as my others. For example, for my book, *Parents Are Lifesavers,* the publisher was paying for the books and all the marketing in their catalog, but my flyers assisted my sales because I was also letting others know about this new product. A librarian in my city took one of my flyers back to a staff meeting, and the Metro Nashville Public Library System ordered my books for all of the libraries in the city.

My marketing plan was so clear and intentional to me that I followed and wrote down what I envisioned. This is the **who, why, what, how and when – the five W's**. Remember, I am sharing my experience of my first book, *Parents Are Lifesavers,* which is used in school districts around the world and is currently being granted permission for reprint by others. In the back of this book will be a

Sample of a Marketing Plan for my book, *Poise for the Runway of Your Life*. I used my one-sheet to market to universities to reach students as well as teachers. I also targeted elementary and secondary schools to reach parents and teachers for my first book. Next, I use my one-sheet for my last three books to market to all universities who teach spirituality and psychology in the world. All of my books can be considered textbooks for student learning. Lastly, I market the same books to metaphysics churches, regular bookstores, traditional churches and their bookstores. The one-sheets can be sent by email in an open email body, not an attachment, since some programs will not open attachments in such a format. I am including a sample in the resources section.

The Book is Live – 1996

I did not stop there once that book went 'live', the term publishers use when a book is printed on time. I ordered about $500 worth of books for marketing and promotions! Because the book had a barcode and ISBN, which is the identification of a book, and a major publisher, I could get the book into libraries and major bookstores. A book can be published without the identification of an ISBN. However, one must understand a product cannot get into major stores and libraries unless it has the product identification. They cost about $125 per code. If you want to become your own publisher, you can look on-line under www.ISBN.org. Most self-publishers or publishers have their own ISBN numbers. There are disadvantages and advantages to becoming your own publisher or not. One disadvantage is that it will cost you more money and time to set everything up for ownership. Nonetheless, when you own your rights to all publishing materials, you reap all monetary benefits, 100% profit. While on the subject, a copyright protects your work. When working with a self-publisher or publisher, they will get it for you. A copyright may be in your name or the publisher's. A copyright can be obtained by mail or on-line; do a search on www.uscopyright.com and also learn about publishing laws. A copyright, if you want to be your own publisher, is around $35. My book with Corwin Press is their ISBN and copyright; I was the author.

I have no ownership to that book except I receive yearly royalties. My other books are self-published. For now, the ISBN is not mine, but I own full ownership of those books. I still receive royalties every three months. I chose this route instead of a vanity press, which is using a press where I would have to have everything ready to print. In self-publishing, they may provide editing, marketing, design and layout, and more for a fee. You can choose to go the route I took and hire your own people. For example, I will have a resource of people listed that I use. When I self-publish, I make a small payment for four months while I am still writing. Then, I pick a cover from stock, or for the last book, I chose a custom cover. They have to get the cover on the internet sites, blogs, build a person website, book layout, and everything to get it ready. This includes all marketing and promotions, seek on-line bookstores, etc. A publisher like Corwin Press is a traditional publisher. When I choose this route, I do not have to have a business license, buy ISBN #'s, hire a printer, or do all the publishing work myself. On the other hand, the one who chooses to self-publish keeps all the money. No matter which route you seek, please enter into prayer and seek guidance. Then, seek an attorney for literary advice, contracts, and publishing laws. If you are one who does not want to publish right away, but wants to use a traditional publisher like the Penguin Group, etc., you will need a query, a literary agent for representation. Most publishers will not read anything from you without a literary agent. A notable exception, however, is a new traditional publisher like Westry Wingate Group who will look at your manuscript(s) without the need for an intermediate agent. If you do end up seeking representation, you can do a search on the Internet for the type of book you are seeking to write, in order to contact those literary agents specializing in what you're writing about. Then, you must follow the directions of the requirements for the query. If you contact a query by email, the letter or package must be opened in the body of the email; do not send an attachment. The agent's directions may require regular mail. They may ask you to send a stamped, self-addressed envelope. The agent will not open it. Be sure to follow the detailed instructions. Once you receive a contract, if they sell your manuscript, they will receive a percentage. This, again, is when you should seek literary counsel. I will include a letter of query in the resources at the back of this book.

You must know publishers want to know the aspiring authors platform for his book. For example, I love inspiring others to write their books; for those who think they cannot do it. So, I teach classes at centers, churches, write articles on the subject, and charge a fee that is reasonable and comfortable for the participant. They also want to know if the aspiring author is using social media, following over five thousand, and have a website functioning to sell their products. When one queries, the publisher wants to know their event listings and how many people attend. There are many questions they want answers to, but they need to know how you are being marketed and promoted before the book is published. The days are gone when an author does nothing but write and show up at events. The author must be willing to sell their books and make a presence on the internet.

More Work To Do

Once I ordered the books, I started to contact booksellers to buy my book and to allow me to do a signing. Often in this process, one may have to mail a book out for review, which is called promotions; getting the word out. Nonetheless, this will cost you more, especially if you are unknown in the field you are pursuing. In the long run, it will pay off. To get my name out, I sold books to the booksellers without making a profit. Next, I tried to find a venue that was related to my books, like a radio or TV talk show program that related to the same topics as my books. Then, I looked for similar publication to get them to write stories about my book and my work. Again, this was done in 1995-1996, before the new rules of marketing on the Internet.

Lethia Owens: Personal Branding Strategist

Over a year ago, I took a class at the National Speaker's Association's Winter Conference. I would like to share part of the class with you with permission from Lethia Owens. The presenter was the smart Speaker, Author, and Coach, Lethia Owens. You may visit her at www.LethiaOwens.com. Her belief, while I am convinced is true, is that a person or company must be bold, stand out, and get noticed. I have written many books and articles. My last three are helping others make a spiritual and personal transformation. Yet, she had to point out to me that I did not have a personal brand. She went to my website and did not see it. I knew it in my heart, but it was not there. After she shared with me that I did not have a personal brand, I went home and searched for "spiritual and personal transformation" (the niche market for my brand). Guess what, my dears? She was right! I was not located on that search of any Internet search engine. Lethia taught me how to make a newsletter and build an irresistible "Personal Brand."

I recommend the book, *The New Rules of Marketing and PR,* by David Meerman Scott. What is your brand for your product or business? Marketing and public relations have changed their look since the Internet came on the scene, according to Meerman. People will visit your website for information, interaction, and choice; you should give this to them using the power of the Internet.

The Steps I Took Toward Personal Branding:

- First, I changed my website to say, "Are you ready for a Spiritual and Personal Transformation?"
- Next, I asked my website guru to list me on a search engine as fast as he could under the name, (you got it), "Spiritual and Personal Transformation."
- I wrote a newsletter the next day for my website entitled, (you are right again), "Are you ready for a Spiritual and Personal Transformation?"

Lethia taught us to post newsletters; for example, on *EZine Article Directories*. I posted my newsletter there with my keywords (which you know by now.) Only write 500-800 words. Use this article for future talk shows or handouts. I have included a newsletter I use in the resource guide in the back of this book. Lethia taught us how to convert that newsletter into .pdf format and post it on www.Scribd.com. Then, she taught us how to make it into a PowerPoint presentation and upload it to www.Slideshare.net. We use keywords in the title, description, and tags. Last, she suggested I make small, 2-3 minute videos to post on YouTube.com. Check me out on YouTube.com under my name, Carol S. Batey. All of these postings are basically free, they just take time!

"Between saying and doing many a pair of shoes are worn out."
- Italian Proverb

The Success Journey

Henry Ford stated, *"The whole secret of a successful life is to find out what it is one's destiny to do, and then do it."* We create our dreams, we write and sing, see our visions, or paint, cook, sew, build, speak, teach; some of us hear our projects, and we work hard to pay for the projects. God sends us the right people to assist us; Angels, Sages, Saints, and the Spirit of God guides and directs our path. What, then, are we afraid of?

The foreword of *The Science of Mind Textbook*, by Dr. Ernest Holmes, states:

> I do not claim to have discovered any new Truth. The Truth has been known in every age by a few, but the great mass of people has never dreamed that we live in a mental and spiritual world. Today, however there is a great inquiry into the deeper meaning of life because the race has reached a state of unfoldment where a broader scope is possible. (2007, p. 11)

"Fear is nothing more than the negative use of faith," said by Ernest Holmes. The power of your dreams starts with the creative thought, faith, work, the power of imagination, desire, a vision deep inside of something you were born to do, and be dedicated to and committed. Dreams can help you; they can give you direction, increase your potential, and help you to grow and develop, and seize the moment. One must set their priorities for their hopes and dreams to come to fruition. Are you willing to "let go" of fear? Can you put a value on your writing dreams, marketing, promotions and destiny? Can you start this day creating a marketing and promotion plan for your projects? You are a successful entrepreneur writer.

I tried so many times to leave this out, dear reader, but I could not. You are to read this and ponder about using your imagination to tap into God's for creativity:

The Science of Mind Textbook

> Imagination taps the very roots of being and utilizes the same Power that bought the worlds forth from Chaos. "The worlds were framed by the word of God." Imagination is the power of the word, while will is the directive agency denoting the purpose for which the word is spoken. Man reproduces the power to create, and in his own life, control his destiny through the activity of his word. This word cannot be willed, but it can be imagined, of imaged forth, into expression. (2007, p. 126)

Summary

Your project may be done or not. However, *marketing* and *promotions* is where the work starts from branding, social media connections across the world, direct services, book or project trailers, blogs, one-on-one, and more. It is time to overcome fear and rejections, which is part of the publishing world. You will hear NO more than "YES!" Learning and practicing how to align yourself with Higher Power, you will receive insights to know what to do and when. Put a "plan in place." Be open to new and better ideas and step into your destiny! The world is giving you many opportunities, go for them and "get your message" out to the world. Learn how to use the Internet for marketing. Let go of people, places, things, and negative thoughts about your destiny. Move into what you desire, and you are the creator and writer of your life. Use your metaphysical affirmation daily and apply faith.

Meditation for Writers

This morning when I look out my office window, I see and hear nature. I welcome God's signs of winter, after which comes spring, a newness. I see snowy rooftops, icicles on barren tree limbs. Animals search for water and food. I throw out an old piece of chicken and popcorn and the birds love it. The snow is so heavy and crunchy when you walk. Everything is white and bright. This is just a season; everything in this life will change.

Let us pause and see the scene. Picture a blanket of white snow all over your city. Time has stopped. So has your mind. People are living in the *Now!* They must deal with this weather now, not tomorrow, but today. You must deal with your marketing today and tomorrow. Can you enter into a silence of nothing? Let the chatter go within your mind. Then your mind will be still and quiet. Use your imagination to see the sun beaming light from the heavens, all colors, the sky radiating the earth. You can do it. Think nothing. Do nothing. Hear nothing. Breathe big breaths of air and let it out from your belly! Now, ask the God of your understanding how may you serve the world with your project? Wait. Be still and do nothing. Sit in a posture of receiving. Then ask for guidance and direction toward your marketing and promotions. Again, sit still and do nothing. Open your hands, palms up to the sky to be filled from the overflow of the universe. Know that all answers and directions will be given unto you according to your Faith in the Spirit. Just like the birds on a snowy day that eat, pray, sing, play, and fly in faith, so can we! So be it!

MY THOUGHTS AND PRAYERS

"Thoughts unspoken are not unknown to the Divine Mind.
Desire is prayer; and no loss can occur from trusting God with
our desires, that they may be moulded and exalted before they
take form in words and in deeds."

~Mary Baker Eddy, founder of Christian Science
(Science and Health with Key to the Scriptures, 1875, p. 1)

Take the time here to write down your thoughts. Remember, they are prayers as well.

Thomas Edison (1847-1931)

Do you know his story? I really did not know all of it until I went to www.about.com. His hard work paid off for him, a man who only went to school for four months of his life. Edison, a businessman, proficient author, inventor, and scientist, was home schooled by his mother before it was popular. His mother was told he needed to leave school because he was an idiot. His knowledge was gained by reading books and seeking the intelligence in books. He failed 10,000 times before he invented the light bulb. It took Edison five years to create the light bulb. However, Ben Franklin figured out how to use it. One of Thomas's obstacles was that he had shoddy supplies and not enough money. We all have obstacles that are presented in our world when we are trying to invent and create our projects. We learn from the "life lessons" of this great man and inventor. "Whether you think that you can, or that you can't you are usually right" in the words of Mr. Edison! Do you think you can write and finish your book?

Henry Ford (1863-1947)

Was he ordinary or proficient, talented, and gifted? Even after a few years of elementary school, he showed a mechanical aptitude to excel in life. He never went to higher education. At an early adult age, he developed his concepts about cars. He built his first one in his garage at home in 1896. Afterward, he developed and is credited with producing the V-8 engine. He told his engineer about his *vision.* The engineer told him twice it could not be done. Six month later, because of Ford's persistence, it was created.

People made mistakes thinking that Ford was not "*educated.*" (Hill, et. al 2007, p. 54) In *The Prosperity Bible,* people do not understand the word education. The word education is derived from the Latin root word "*educo,*" which means to draw out and develop from within. According to Ford, a man is educated if he "*knows where to get knowledge when he needs it, and how to organize that knowledge into definite plans of action.*" (Hill, et. al, *The Prosperity Bible* 2007, p. 55) Ford created a "Master Mind" group to help him locate the specialized knowledge that he

Chapter 9

Talented and Smart - That's Who You Are!

"Genius is one percent inspiration, ninety-nine percent perspiration."
~Thomas Edison (1863-1947)

As a metaphysical teacher helping my students, I love to inspire and empower them to write their projects! I encounter countless people who cross my path, whether from a radio show or someone who have read my books. In my classes, students have various excuses for not beginning to write. I ask, *"Why Aren't You Writing*?" In communication with them I say, *"Your book is already written; you just need some quiet time to let the book come to you and through your soul."* Afterwards, I still hear excuses like, I do not know how to use a computer; I cannot spell; or at age thirty, a person just taught me how to read. Then, I have the students who are educated, talented and have the "know how", but who just put it off until one day. Another person will share they are just not as disciplined as others. I chose to call all of the student writers "talented and smart" with a story line that can impact the world. During my case studies, I see that the Universal God uses everyone who is willing to share their gifts, talents, and abilities. Everybody has a valuable and a spiritual message to the world. When one tells me they cannot spell, I have bought them dictionaries. On the other hand, when they tell me they cannot use a computer, I have found assistance for them to get their stories on paper. The most important statement for my students and you to know is that your book is already done within one's soul. Just do a "spiritual practice" and seek "silence" and the book will come through you! One must let go of people, places and things in order to achieve their desire to write.

Kim's Story

As a child, Kim was sexual abused daily by her grandfather and uncle. This abuse occurred for ten years. Kim is now 30 years old and has five children by her grandfather and uncle, relatives. The children suffered no mental or physical disabilities from being related to their fathers. Even when Kim told someone about the abuse, it still occurred. Later, Kim started to use drugs and gave her body to the opposite as well as same sex. She is now mentally and physically disabled; she has suffered a stroke and more. Nevertheless, you can see Kim has a story to tell. She heard my radio program and called me to say she wanted to write her story. I said, "My dear, what is keeping you?" Her answer, "I do not know how to spell or use a computer." I shared with her how I wrote, *"Parents Are Lifesavers"* by hand and needed to hire a technical editor to clean and polish up my manuscript. My advice for her was to do hand writing in notebooks and get the story lines that were inside her out and on paper. She did. She wrote four notebooks, and then I found someone to type up her work. She is now getting monetary assistance from the government for her medical issues, and her children are all doing well in church and school.

Joyce's Affair

One day, while at the gym, I posted my flyer for my writing class. Joyce signed up and attended. Her story went like this: While she was in an unhappy marriage, she had an affair with a married man. One day, this man was at Joyce's home, and his wife and children were outside knocking on her door. Joyce's children were not home, and they did not know about her affair. His wife threatened to kick in the door while the children were screaming for their dad. Joyce is now writing her story to say, "There is a better way when you are in a bad marriage; turn to God." She does not wish her situation on anyone. She has learned her lesson now. Before this knowledge, she continued to see him for two more years in their secret hiding places such as cheap motels and such. Joyce was addicted to him, and he was addicted to her. Now, she writes to share her secret with her family and the world. She does not know how to use Microsoft Word so she is hand writing her story as well. The first draft of her book is finished. It is now time for her rewrite and polish! I also gave her resources to find someone to type her book!

Sexual Abuse Stories

Even though my student writers see that I am the metaphysical teacher, they also see I can relate to them as well. I was sexually abused when I was five years old. I tell this story in the classroom. This abuse left me very impressionable, thinking this was the way of life. No one taught me about boundaries. Then, I share the story about my son being in a juvenile home at age sixteen. I was not only worried about him, but also the fact that the woman who molested me worked there. I called her on the phone to solicit her help. She helped me get my son out. Now, it is time for me to share about the "gift of forgiveness." With that being said, I know that others had forgiven me. As I continue to share with the class, there was no way that I could have made that call if I had bitterness in my heart for that woman. She helped get my son out by finding him a public defender in the next courtroom. His father hired an attorney. However, he would never show up for court. I shared this information with her, and she assisted my family and me. More information about this situation is detailed in my third book, *"Poise for the Runway of Your Life"*. (2009) You need to make sure that if you wish to write about this type of abuse or any other, that you have truly forgiven yourself and those involved. You cannot still hold anger towards the Creator who made you.

Jennifer Speaks

This educated, talented, cute woman was amazed. Her amazement was that I could candidly stand before a class of people I did not know and share my story. Subsequently, she confessed her story of being sexually abused by her uncle for nine years. Then, another man spoke up and talked about his mother sexually abusing him and shaming him for ten years. Jennifer stood up and spoke to the class to say, "Look at this teacher. She is beautiful and well dressed." Jennifer needed to see a woman like me who could tell her story in front of others without any emotions and fears. Jennifer is now writing her sexual abuse story to impact others' lives that face and experience this type of trauma. Her message is that there is hope for those people to live a productive life after being sexually abused.

Jesse Starts

Jesse came to my class when I shared my sexual abuse story and he said, "I question God; why did this have to happen?" At that moment, I say to Jesse, "Do not question God anymore. Just write it all out on paper and the answers will float into your mind." Therefore, things happen to us for our growth in this life to get over, move on, and reach back and help another person. Such was my case and others. Write it out, and the peace of understanding will happen in due season. He is from South America, and he can barely speak English. Nonetheless, he is slowly writing his story. Jesse is writing his truth the way he sees it. He is writing.

Rhonda Hudson, a middle-aged, laid off corporate worker, took my webinar class on *Why Aren't You Writing? Unlocking Your Potential to Write.* This student wrote the following creative piece. She submitted it to her city paper in Cleveland, Ohio and it was published.

"Laid Off or Liberated?"

August 10, 2010

by Rhonda Hudson

At this time, the country is experiencing 9.5 percent of folks unemployed. More and more people are out of work longer and longer. The number of people out of work for more than six months rose by 169,000 to 6.9 million, which is 45.9 percent of all the unemployed. With so many people not working, people are starting to rely on themselves for their own security and tapping into skills they have not used. There seems to be a movement of "I can depend on myself to take care of myself. I want to control my own destiny." Being laid off can be used as a time of relaxation, reflection, and freedom. Not having to concern one's self with setting the clock, upper management issues, and fighting traffic, one can become free. After being laid off, I had an opportunity to meet up with some former employees who had also been laid off. After not seeing them for a while, I noticed how relaxed everyone's face looked. I realized the stress had showed itself on all of our faces while employed and going through the motions of being downsized before our layoff came. After being laid off, we were all fresh faced. There is a term being used now called "fun employment." People are starting to not allow the stress get to them and are realizing there is something better waiting for them, whether they create their own job or find another. Being unemployed has caused a spiritual awakening in some and a lot have found they are not out of work, but on a spiritual journey. Unemployment can open up our creative selves.

In the meantime, have fun, do some things having a 9 to 5 would not allow. Pull out those crochet needles, write your book, pull up whatever it is that has been buried inside you and create. Unemployment is not an end, it is a beginning.

Rhonda is now going back to school studying Public Relations. Then, she can use her skills to write for herself and others. You too can learn to write or to apply your skills to write to assist others.

Ordinary People

We all have work and a mission to do in this lifetime. The sufferings we have suffered are learning lessons to be put into perspective and to be for giving to others. Most want to bury the pain, abuse, affairs, neglect, trauma, etc., under the rug and hide it away. I say write about it; give it a voice. Use the negative for a positive result and help yourself first and then another person. Maybe you are to publish it, speak on the topic, write a play or a poem about it, or just write about it and release it to the Universal God. Then you will be able to let it go and let God. You are not ordinary; you are gifted and talented beyond all means. Write your story. Start here and finish in a notebook, personal computer, or recording device.

____

____

____

____

____

____

____

____

needed to become one of the richest and most successful men of his time. This practice, "Master Mind" group is carried out throughout history. This man prided himself on his persistence. Although he began his life poor and so called uneducated, he died a philanthropist. He never gave up on his dreams. He used the information within his mind to make his dreams a reality, and so can you, my dear writer.

Think and Grow Rich

You can become a successful entrepreneur writer by using the 13 principles founded by Napoleon Hill in his book, *Think and Grow Rich*. I am going to take the 13 principles and relate them to building a successful career in writing:

- **Thoughts are Things**

Hill taught that once our thoughts are combined with purpose, persistence, and burning desire, they can be converted into money and material goods. So, you want to write; that is your purpose. Other words for persistence are determination and diligence. Do you have the determination and diligence to get up early or to stay up late to finish your book? When I write my book, I cannot stop that which is a burning desire.

- **Desire**

The first step for writing starts with desire. How bad do you want to write a book? Are you ready for success? Do you let doubts, fears, and worry cause you to fall?

- **Faith**

In my classes, I pass out a mustard seed. It is the smallest of all the plants, yet it yields one of the biggest plants. Dear writer, you must exercise faith in order to become successful. Can you see your dreams and desires in order to achieve your destiny to write books? Faith is a "state *of mind that may be induced by auto-suggestion.*" (Hill, et.al, 2007 p. 38)

- **Auto-Suggestion**

Your metaphysical affirmations for writing that you created in this book are positive statements that are true, such as auto-suggestions. If you fix your thoughts on what you would like to achieve, you will be able to achieve it.

- **Specialized Knowledge**

Everyone on this planet has general (regular) and specialized knowledge. If you are lacking specialized knowledge in using a computer or spelling, you can find someone to help you succeed. Put a plan into action like Henry Ford when he pushed his engineer to persist with the building of the V-8 motor. Ford did not act alone. The idea is to use a "Master Mind" group to gather specialized knowledge required to succeed. This concept was developed in the 1800's. There is assistance for book writing out there; you must humbly seek it.

- **Imagination**

Albert Einstein was a physicist most famous for his theories of relativity for which he won the Nobel Prize. He is also famous for stating, "*Imagination is far more important than knowledge. For knowledge is limited to all we now know and understand, while imagination embraces the entire world, and all there ever will be to know and understand.*" (Thinkexist.com) The ability to image something must be present before one can create something. Before writing anything, I would sit and visualize myself writing and speaking to my readers.

- **Organized Planning**

In order to write books, speak, teach, and create, one must have a "plan to action." Henry Ford became a successful businessman when he developed an organized "plan to action" and did not give up on the creation of the V-8 motor. Most of my writing students have great ideas. They are not focused enough on one idea to bring that one to pass. Focus on one idea and organize a "plan to action." I have included a sample "plan to action" in the resources section of this book.

- **Decision**

Many of us fail to become successful writers because we postpone important decisions or make poor decisions instead of taking the time to examine all of our options. "*Procrastination, the opposite of decision, is a common enemy which practically every man must conquer.*" (Hill, et al, 2007, p.103) As you make a decision for writing, follow your "plan to action," stick to it, and move forward. Do not let others delay your decision- making process to write your projects.

- **Persistence**

You must be persistent within your soul when pursuing your dreams. If you allow setbacks and mistakes from your past to hinder you, you will never move forward into your writing goals. Have faith and apply it daily.

- **Power of the "Master Mind" Group**

The *Master Mind* is defined as the *"coordination of knowledge and effort, in a spirit of harmony, between 2 or more people, for the attainment of a definite purpose."* (Hill, et al, 2007, p. 124) This process requires you to work with others to achieve your dreams and theirs. Most people, when they read a book, think the author, no matter who he/she is, worked alone. The author most likely relied on others for help in the compilation, editing, research, formatting, and publication of his book. It is my belief that all authors, even bestselling authors, seek assistance from others in order to shed light on how to improve their works. I know I do!

- **The Mystery of Sex Transmutation**

The words simply mean a change from one form to another. Hill refers to sexual transmutation as a "*switching of the mind from thoughts of physical expression of human desires...to thoughts of some other nature*". (Hill, et al, 2007, p. 128) Once you get a burning desire to create books within your soul, you will experience the discovery of imagination, courage, will, persistence, and creative forces that you never knew you had!

- **The Subconscious Mind**

Your subconscious mind knows your deepest fears, desires, and beliefs. When you practice faith and utilize metaphysical affirmations, your subconscious mind will recognize these positive forces and begin making positive changes within one's soul and life.

- **The Brain**

Drs. Alexander Graham and Elmer R. Gates observed that every human brain, in order to write a new project, sits and visualizes the work coming through and then starts it.

"Success comes to those who are success conscious." -Napoleon Hill (1883-1970)

Summary

So, you want to write your project. The book project is already written; it was written long before you came to earth. Can you go into a state of quite meditation and silence? You are gifted and talented; you have the ability to write. Maybe you have been told you are "just an ordinary" writer or person. The same was said of Edison and Ford. They both had so-called lack of education, yet they both used their metaphysical power within to soar. They had a mission to be accomplished for the world. Do not let the limitations you have given yourself stop you from becoming a prolific writer. Do you understand your purpose in this life? Follow your inspirations and hunches, and create a *Master Mind* group. Create your "plan to action" and a "timeline" and follow it to the letter of the law.

Meditation for Writers

Right now, let us enter into the silence of nothings. I am hearing outside the birds singing. It is ringing like music in my ears and soul. Say to yourself, I am talented and gifted. I can do what God is calling me to do. This is my mission to write to the world; I said "YES!" before coming to this earth. I hear no rejection about my writing. My book is done. I just need to sit quietly and let the words flow into my brain for others to read. I have suffered enough and learned my "life lessons." I am answering the call to write books. Let us enter into silence this day to hear those words to write. So it is!

My Thoughts And Prayers

"Thoughts unspoken are not unknown to the Divine Mind. Desire is prayer; and no loss can occur from trusting God with our desires, that they may be moulded and exalted before they take form in words and in deeds."

~Mary Baker Eddy, founder of Christian Science
(Science and Health with Key to the Scriptures, 1875, p. 1)

Take the time here to write down your thoughts. Remember, they are prayers as well.

Chapter 10
Writing to Create and Beyond

"If there's a book you really want to read, but it hasn't been written yet, then you must write it.
~Toni Morrison (1931-present)

Is there a book you want to read and it is not published yet? Then it is your job to write it! Are you one who is inspired to *write and create? Do you see, feel, and sense things differently from others?* Are you able to express yourself through music, art, the spoken word, dance, poetry, designing clothing, sculpture, writing, film, acting, or other types of activities? How quickly do you translate what you see into emotional feelings that transfer into the written word? There are so many ways of expressing the gifts that the Universal God has given us. However, this chapter's focus is on the talents of *"creative writing."* Maybe your gifts of *"creative writing"* are novels, short stories, non-fiction, fiction, poetry, screenwriting, children's books, play writing, personal essays, family history, autobiographical journal writing, etc. If you are not a professional journalist, but you use your talents as a writer without the technical literary aspects, you are probably practicing *"creative writing."* There are many high schools and universities that offer *"creative writing"* courses. While the major focus is *"creative writing,"* students still learn traditional studies such as math, science, physical education, art, technology, history, foreign language, English, and more. (www.insideschools.org)

"Writing is both mask and unveiling."
-E. B. White (1899-1985)

Creative Writing in Schools

Presently, there are now many higher education academic schools that offer Bachelor and Master's degrees in fine art degrees. On the other hand, there are on-line courses one may enroll in and you do not have to leave your home. (www.creativewriting.com) In local communities at-large, there are a host of classes and workshops offered to enhance the technical issues of editing, structural writing techniques, writers block, peer and teacher critique. Within the classes or workshops, a writer may improve their writing process. A participant's written work may be evaluated by others (peers) for the points of view in the story, dialogue, how the characters play out, the theme, setting of the story, and more. Often the writer is encouraged to write, edit, rewrite, edit, and then polish their work by teachers. There are many literary benefits. One benefit is the writer shares his or her course work, enhances his imagination, and gets positive feedback from others. This critique is not about good or so-called "bad" writing. It is about improving the story lines to better impact the person who is reading the book.

"To avoid criticism, do nothing, say nothing, and be nothing."
~Elbert Hubbard (1856-1915)

My goal as a metaphysical inspirational motivator is for you to start to unlock your creativity to write your projects. Your job is to take paper and pen or a computer and write. Then, set time aside to write every day for about 30 minutes at first. Then, build up to an hour, and then 2 hours. Begin with the creative writing exercise on the following page...

Creative Writing EXERCISE 1:

You are to look at the clock. You may set it but give yourself ten minutes to write about the following subjects.* Convert your feelings into thoughts and your thoughts into words. Your written tone for the exercises may be reflective, interesting, believable, inspirational, sad, or happy. Do not over analyze your feelings while writing the exercise. To learn more about Creative Writing, read the book *"The Creative Writing Course"* **by Julia Bell and Pave Magrs.**

*** Picture of a person doing yoga on the beach, the sun is just coming up and it is warm outside.**

____

____

____

____

____

____

____

____

____

***The Shape of a Diamond**

How did that expression of *"creative writing"* process make you feel? The exercise was created to help you improve your expressions of thought and improve your writing craft.

Create a Context that will Allow People to Think

"The skill of writing is to create a context in which other people can think."
~Edwin Schlossberg (1945-present)

Your job as a writer in the field of non-fiction is helping your reader answer their important questions. As I have said before, if the reader spends their time and means to buy your book, they want results and insights to their life questions and to be inspired. Many of your readers will need inspiration to be educated, entertained. They desire results to their inner struggles and challenges. Keep in mind, you are building a personal relationship with your readers that may last for a long-time. I write sequels of books that answer the same questions in all of my books except this one. The questions I had in my mind before were, "what is needed for them to learn from, and how would I present the material to the reader in a way that they could grasp it into their knowledge?" In addition, before I write, I must understand and know the value of my writing to my reader. That way, I can keep them reading my literary works and keep a lasting relationship with them. My intentions are to enlighten my readers on what they may have felt was missing in their life, world, and affairs. Further, it is my job as a sequel writer to inform, give value to my reader's life, and build trust in exchange for my lasting relationship with my reader. The results are my books are being bought over and over again! I am giving them or someone they know step-by step answers to their daily living and personal challenges. Remember my brand, a "spiritual and personal transformation." Always keep in mind your mission, purpose, intention, and branding for your writing when starting to write. Know your ideal reader; see them. Visualize that reader on the beach after doing their yoga and lying on a towel reading your book. What do you want the reader to know before they read or listen to your materials? Readers have all types of learning styles: visual, hearing and touch. Be sure, dear writer, that you touch all those types within your book or project.

A Diamond in the Rough

Your Manuscript should be crucial advice and information. It should be significant written material that you are giving the reader. You want to develop a lasting impression on the reader. It is essential that you, the writer, give *clear* and *intentional* information to the reader for their life. In my last book, I integrated live food recipes into the storylines. If I had left out one single ingredient, when the reader put it together, the recipe would not have come out right. Steps for the recipes were formulated and then everything was blended together to create a valuable creation. Your main purpose while putting the chief words on paper is to formulate a worthy creation that the reader can apply to their life and use. If you are writing a self-help book, a worthy creation of guidebooks, textbooks, or inspirational books, give the reader steps of "how they can improve their lives or the lives of others." Make the writing process simple for your target reader and build a long-term readership with them. The consequences of the lasting relationship are that they will tell others, and they will continue to buy other books. The results will be your books will fly off the shelf, your website, social media or other forms of *on-line bookstores* like BarnesandNoble.com, etc. My dear writer, you do realize that storefront bookstores are closing; the Internet and *on-line bookstores* are the future. I cannot advocate this enough if you are one who does not understand how to use the Internet for marketing and reaching the buyer. Please take classes or hire someone to do it for you.

Now, if you are writing worthy fiction, you are entertaining, educating, humoring, and delighting their interest. You too must know your principle ideas in your story lines to communicate to your reader and keep them coming back for more, like J. K. Rowling, the author of the *Harry Potter* series. She writes follow-up books and films, which are sequels. Look at her life now after writing so many books, which were then turned into screenplays. She kept her dedicated readers coming back for more and more and more ... You too can do the same. That brings an ocean, not a stream, of steady income. Is that what you want as a writer, whether it is non-fiction or fiction? I do! Consequently, one becomes a successful entrepreneur writer. I say "Yes" to that concept and claim the success. *Can you say "Yes" too?*

It has been my experience to "start to think" of how to get my word out about the book and what outcome do I desire of the printed material. Intentional clarity is necessary here as well. I enter into a silence with an intentional goal of reaching the "target market." *I see them*. Consumers are so busy, so I must gain their attention. There are so many books being printed daily. How do I gain their attention? I do not know about you, but I know I have a Power living within me that is Higher than me. *Do you have the same?* I seek guidance and direction from that inner source, that inspirational source, that Divine Guidance. What must I do? Which way do I market? I dedicate my project to that source that is Higher than I. Then humbly I say, show me the way and I surrender and follow. In Chapter 8 of this handbook, it has already been written about marketing and promotion. Nonetheless, one must never forget the process of thinking about "how to get the message out" to the public. Your "creative writing" can be essential in this step for communicating your fundamental ideas to the public to create money. Offer classes, mini workshops, e-courses (that you write and deliver to someone's email), web or teleconferences, or phone classes on Skype (if a person is located in another location), before your book is finished to test the crucial materials and gain a following. Many people are using podcasts (a digital download message that people can purchase for a small price.) You may want to charge a small fee or nothing at all, it is your choice. You can blog about a subject that seems vital to your writing. Do you have something to say and no body to say it too? Then, create a blog or podcast. I always put the introduction and the cover of my books on my website before it goes to print for anyone on site. Once the book is done, you may consider burning a CD or DVD with shared information from the book or a live class. As stated before, consumers are busy. One must reach them wherever they are, in the car, at home, in their office, on their personal computer, Kindle, iPod, Touchpad, etc. If you have a website or perhaps are on a social network, offer a free download of three chapters of an e-book or a percentage off coaching or a class. Build and maintain a trust and get in contact with your reader. You get the picture, don't you? Your job is imperative to create oceans of income from your product and services offered to your readers. Books are a means to getting into the consumers life. Then, it is of the upmost importance that you stay connected with them and create additional products to sell to them. People do not increase their income alone on books; they create other services to sell. This concept has been going on for a long time. Motivational speakers make a large amount of their money on products and their services rather than their book sales.

As a "creative non-fiction writer," your job is to weave "answer threads" of inspiration into a torn life of the dedicated readers. Remember, your spiritual and personal journey is your transformation from chaos to a clear pathway. What helped you get through the "darkness of your soul?" What were the critical elements you could leave your readers? After you came through the indispensable darkness and pain, what was your life-lesson? What strength and courage did you gain? Share that vital information with your dear readers. Do not leave any keys out of the material; it may be the one key needed by the reader. Your work is spiritual, whether it is non-fiction or fiction. It is all channeled by a Higher Power, so learn to listen within your soul. Ask, "What were the needs of my soul?" The message is of the essence to your reader and yourself. If you are the writer, you are probably your greatest teacher and reader first. Do you agree? I write books I wished I had read while I was doing the project or going into a "dark night" within my soul and life. Everyone on this earth needs encouragement, delight, entertainment, and instruction.

Creative Writing EXERCISE 2:

Before you do these exercises, enter into a silence, seeking a Higher Power's direction. You want to create writing, whether it is non-fiction or fiction, which will allow the reader to think, provide answers to their weighty, inner questions that maybe they have not asked anyone; to educate, entertain, answer questions, delight, and inspire the reader to action. There is no storyline except the one you create. All the while, you are writing, keep your mission, intention, and purpose clear in your soul. See the reader. Go back to the Subtitle.

Create content that will allow people to think. Re-read that section and ponder it's meaning before you write here. I want you to write a poem, words to a song, a play, a story line, non-fiction, or fiction here on the spaces provided. Do not worry about the content you are writing; this is your time to be creative.

____

____

____

____

____

____

____

____

Dear Writer,

It is my hope and prayer that you found wisdom in between the storylines of this handbook that was created for you! I wish I had this material 17 years ago! Nonetheless, you have it now. I am not an English teacher; I am a motivator, an inspirational teacher or coach, a guiding force for you to learn from. There are many classes available on-line or in person for you to sharpen your "**creative writing.**" If you look on-line at www.creativewritingcourses.com, you will find whatever you desire. If you are one who wants to be educated further in *"creative writing" or "writing in general,"* seek a school of Higher Learning. There are courses on-line or in a university. Remember that creative writing is to provoke and captivate your reader's thoughts and feelings.

Summary

Remember, dear writer, *"creative writing"* is to provoke and captivate your reader's thoughts and feelings. First, that action must be activated within your soul. Your job is to educate, delight, instruct, and give inspiration. It does not matter if it is pretend, drama, imaginative, enlighten, non-fiction, or fiction. Use your imagination and inner resource skills. You have the creative power that, from Higher Power, is higher when you tap into that Source. Write to help people think and provide inspiring answers to their daily solutions. Do not forget to use your intentional purpose and mission while writing so that you will write into their hearts and soul. Think about what to write about before you come to your place to write. Enter into a silence and seek guidance from that Higher Source. Captivate your readers so that you can build trust and a long-term relationship. Develop other products. Remember an author does not make all his or her money just on books. Can you motivate? Thank you for taking the time to read this material and spending your money to buy this book. You are very important to me. I love you and wish you much success! Please learn how to take your message to the Internet and social media sync.

Meditation for Writers

Yes, my dear writers, there is so much to do to get a book published! Can you say "YES!" to this process, then enter in a silence and surrender? Once you say "YES!" to the Universal God that you are committed to, the process of writing all things will be given unto you.

Right now, enter into a silence, take a breath, and see your finished product. Do you see it? Your project! Breathe a breath of thanksgiving for the accomplishment; you did it. The books or the projects that you are CALLED to do are already done long before you came to this earth. All you have to do is to say "YES!" and surrender to the Universal God and step into the destiny of writing! When you get a so-called writers block, come back to this handbook and re-read the lessons and move forward. You are imperative to the literary world. You have a magnitude of work to be shared with others. You have the inner keys to unlock your potential to write books. So be it!

MY THOUGHTS AND PRAYERS

"Thoughts unspoken are not unknown to the Divine Mind. Desire is prayer; and no loss can occur from trusting God with our desires, that they may be moulded and exalted before they take form in words and in deeds."

~Mary Baker Eddy, founder of Christian Science
(Science and Health with Key to the Scriptures, 1875, p. 1)

Take the time here to write down your thoughts. Remember, they are prayers as well.

PLAN TO ACTION

WHO?	WHAT?	WHEN?	WHERE?	WHY?
WHO are you marketing the materials to?	Need media pitch; find distribution of your project such as brochures, flyers, promotional ideas, e-marketing materials, press releases	Before book the book is completed	Get in on social media; i.e. blogs, podcast, viral marketing, online media	To get YOUR message out!
WHO is your target audience?	Create a book trailer or pay for one	Once you get the book cover	From your office or someone you have hired	To sell YOUR book!
WHO? Local editors, newspapers, or magazines	Book reviews from people of interest, editors, writers	Once the book is completed or once it becomes live	Internet, or your local city publications	To get positive feedback about YOUR project!
WHO is your marketing target? Search the Internet for free reviewers or, pay a small fee	One-sheet and bio for interviews	Once your book becomes live	Print, TV, radio, churches, schools, bookstores, internet media	The one-sheet – should have all the important info included here - This is about YOUR book!

Aspiring Author,

We made it to the end of this book! Wow, how do you feel? Now, you are ready to start the writing process or your creative project. Most people feel they are not ready to write because they have not had any creative writing classes or courses. The most important writing task you have to do is "just write."

I know that your potential to create books is now unlocked. I see you writing daily; you are having a mystical experience and the inner light force is guiding your writing journey. This is your mission, your purpose, to create good books for the world. Whenever you are stuck, and many of you will be, I suggest that you pick up this book again and re-read its' content. Along with that process, be kind to yourself and take one step at a time. Breathe, Breathe, Breathe and take it slow.

I sincerely appreciate that you took the time to read my work and spent your money to buy my book. It was created for you. I love you! Contact me anytime by email: carol37076@aol.com or Facebook/CarolBatey.

I am Grateful,
Author Carol S. Batey

"We Are What We Write."
~Michael Wood nd

"Ms. Carol,
Attending your class, 'Why Aren't Your Writing? Unlocking Your Potential to Write', was the lost key to my future. You taught me to say, 'Yes and Surrender'. Well, I have surrendered and thanks to your giving of yourself, I am an author. Thanks for your awesome gift of words."

~Kimberly Graham-Johnson

RESOURCES FOR WRITERS

EDITING AND PROOFREADING

mlmindy71@gmail.com

Mindy Liska

lfinkcox@gmail.com

Lydia Cox

prideroller@comcast.net

Lolita Pride

djbush@sbcglobal.net

Doris Bush

MARKETING, EDITING, SOCIAL MEDIA ETC.

Emily.heinlen@gmail.com

Emily Heinlen

www.writersinthesky.com

Yvonne Perry

COVER DESIGN

daviddickerson12@gmail.com

David Dickerson

Many self publishers offer stock images.

WEBSITE DESIGN

www.fredrichfinch.com

Fred Finch

FREE ARTICLE LISTINGS

www.freearticlelisting.com

www.selfgrowth.com

www.econnect.entrepreneur.com

www.problogger.net

FREE BOOK REVIEWS

www.rawsistaz.com

www.freebookreview.com

PUBLISHER

www.wwgpress.com

WESTRY WINGATE GROUP

Please do your own research on self-publishers and publishers.

SAMPLE QUERY LETTER

QUERY LETTER

Date

Agent/Publisher name
Address 1
Address 2
City/State Zip Code

Subject: Manuscript Submission Request

Status: Simultaneous submission / Propriety submission. A completed project.

Represented by: Author/Literary Agent

Dear PUBLISHER:

I am requesting permission to submit my manuscripts for your evaluation. The first book, Poise for the Runway of Your Life is 352 pages and has been printed in a limited printing by AuthorHouse in Bloomington, Indiana. The second book, In Due Season: Destiny is Calling Your Soul is 140 pages and has also been printed in a limited printing by AuthorHouse.

Poise for the Runway of Your Life is a guidebook based on my personal story, an insightful journey about re-creating myself in every way - from physical health to career path to personal growth. Through this journey, I recall my childhood destiny to become a model. After raising six children during my 21-year marriage, I reinvented myself. Today, I am a model at the age of 54 and a Spiritual Lifestyle Coach. In Due Season: Destiny is Calling Your Soul is a step-by-step account of my personal transformation that led me to discover my purpose on this Earth and explains how readers can put themselves on the path to their own personal transformation.

The market for these books will be anyone who wishes to reinvent or transform his or her life. This genre has become especially important in today's tough economic times as people are searching now more than ever for their purpose in life. These books are better than others on the market as they are based on a true story. Both books can be considered guidebooks or how-to manuals told in the form of a personal narrative which allows the reader to not only become involved with the story, but to also identify with the characters in such a way as to propel him or herself into action.

Both a #10 SASE for your response and a large SASE for return of the manuscript have been enclosed.

I look forward to hearing from you.

Sincerely,

Carol S. Batey
Suite 203 Lucky Drive
Nashville, TN 37211
Cell: (615) 485-4548
E-mail: carol37076@aol.com
www.artlifestylecoach.com

~

Points to Consider for the Query Letter

- **THE HOOK: (Attention)**
- **THE PITCH: (What you are offering - selling your book)**
- **THE CREDENTIALS: (What gives you the RIGHT to write this book or article?)**
- **THE CLOSER or KICKER: (One more reason to look at your work/represent you)**
- **YOUR CONTACT INFORMATION**

SAMPLE NEWSLETTER

THE LOVE GAME

BY MINISTER OF METAPHYSICS AND LIFESTYLE COACH CAROL S. BATEY

How many of you play sports, sew, cook or anything that has guidelines and rules? What makes the love connection any different for seeking a partner? We often say we are ready for a life-partnership and yet, just because we desire a partnership, does that mean we are going to receive the wish just by saying it? Do you want a Beloved of your own?

Partner or Not

Single people, you have a choice to partner or not. Did you know this? Nowadays, it appears that people aren't getting married as fast as they formerly did, regardless of age. You can attract your Beloved to you. Do you believe that you must be cute, skinny, educated, or rich? Those things are about outer appearances, not an inner quality. Nonetheless, single people often think they are no one unless they are attached to someone. (Gen 1:27), ***"God created man in His own image, in the image of God created He him; male and female created He them."*** Our first partnership should be with God first and then ourselves. Then, maybe we can keep our relationships. Stop speaking negative about relationships, "there's no one on this earth here for me." Then it will be so. What is this process called? The Law of Attraction. If you truly desire a "life partner" then it starts with you and in your own consciousness and with cause and effect.

Take Personal Responsibility

Can you go to work thinking positive about your dreams

of the right partner? Use the gift of imagination; stir the desires and seeds into your consciousness, make you list of what you want. Then, stir into the mix *intention*, which means a purpose in mind. Get yourself, mind, soul, and spirit ready to be noticed for dating and attracting a partner to you. Get out of the house and fix yourself up. Become ready; take up position to seek what type of partnership you desire. Start to mentally, emotionally, socially, and spiritually think how to use your resources to attract your Beloved to you. What are you willing to give for another person? How do you and the other person want to live? Are you looking for a 24-7 type of relationship, or a 3 times a week type of relationship? Be real clear about what your desires are up front, and don't settle for what you need for your soul. Ask your soul what your needs are for a relationship. What type of ministry do you and your partner plan to do? Think, don't rush into a relationship because you feel or think there is no one else out there.

Fear of Getting Hurt

Many single people want their past to be their future. So, are you stuck in the memory of a past relationship? Are you using the past as an excuse of *"I can't be in full time relationship because I got hurt last time."* What about the concept of living in the Now? For all of us today, changing our old patterns of thinking is the only way to create a new relationship pattern today! In the book of Romans (12:2), ***"Do not be conformed to this world, but be transformed by the renewal of your mind, that you may prove what is the will of God what is good and acceptable and perfect."*** Change is very difficult for people. However, if one would change their thinking to a more positive thought, then their world would change to a positive world.

From My Book, *What's Cooking in Your Soul?*

Can you let go of fear, doubt and worry? If you would like to try, turn the old relationship over to God. What did you learn from the experiences? Take the good and the not so good and move into the Now. Ask God for the type of partner you desire and then release the outcome, the when and how. Trust the Universal God for the right timing. Next, set your intentions on what kind of partnership you want to create; see it, live it and be it. Wait now in a spirit of expectancy. Practice prayer and meditation to draw the right relationship to you in due season.

Put an Action Plan in Place. Get out of the house, fix yourself up, become more social and move…into the world. Can you follow God's prompting to act? When one door closes many will be open unto you. Wait upon the God. Be your inner love coach. Lastly, give thanks to the Universal God for blessings unfolding on your behalf …

From Rev. Eric Ovid Donaldson, Senior Minister, Unity Christian Church, Memphis, TN:

"As a minister who, at this minute, has several books stirring within me, I applaud Carol Batey not only for doing what I have not yet done, but for how she has done so; by following the dictates of the Spirit. Carol is a whirlygig of energy and ideas, expressing freely and purposefully. She is clear about the opportunities presenting themselves, but only wishes to do so genuinely in sincere service to the Spirit and to others.

Her latest offering, *Why Aren't You Writing? Unlocking Your Potential to Write Books* inspires me. The book chronicles Batey's creative process. It helps simplify my creative process, in the process. Anyone who aspires to write can get tremendous value out of each step Ms. Batey recounts. She reinforces each chapter with memorable quotes and masterful insights. I recommend this book to both new and seasoned writers. For novices, Batey offers ways to develop discipline and follow through. For seasoned writers, Batey's creativity and perspective can effectively dissolve any writer's blocks one may be experiencing.

Personally I am more confident than I have ever been about authoring a book this year. Thank you, Carol, for unlocking my potential to write books."

From Yvonne Perry, author of Whose Stuff is This?:

"Goals, plan, prayer, and action! This workbook is the perfect blend of spiritual knowledge and instruction on the craft of writing. Learn to write from the inspiration of your heart and divine guidance!"

SAMPLE ONE SHEET

New Release: *What's Cooking in Your Soul?*

Author: Carol S. Batey
www.artlifestylecoach.com – 615-485-4548
carol37076@aol.com

Areas of Interest:
Book Clubs
Wellness
Lifestyle
Churches
Colleges
Motivational

Speaking Topics:
Spirituality
Dreaming Dreams
Motivational
Fitness and Health
Spiritual and Personal Transformations

Available:
Amazon.com
Target.com
Authorhouse.com
E-book
Tower.com
Borders.com
Barnes and Noble.com
Ingram
Baker and Taylor

For discounted books see: newleaf.com

Date Published: October 2010 - Publisher: Authorhouse - Paperback: 178 pages - ISBN: 1449034497

Sample Marketing Plan, Part 1

Outline for Success - Carol Batey

Project: Poise for the Runway of Your Life: Spiritual Self-Help Book

Goal: The primary goal for this marketing campaign is to create national awareness of the book and Carol Batey through media interviews, reaching out to the colleges that teach spirituality and psychology and workshops (churches, women's organizations) from the radio listening audiences, which will translate into sales and also get the attention of a publisher.

Target: Demographic: Women 35-54

SAMPLE MARKETING PLAN, PART 2

Poise for the Runway of Your Life
Up, Up, and Away We Go!

Marketing and Promotion

•Poise for the Runway of Your Life
•Press release to be written for national press and also the New Thought press, i.e. Unity, Science of Mind, etc. Reach out to New Thought Distribution and other outlets like Vision Distribution. DONE
•Develop press kit to include an attention getting item so that the appropriate people will at least look at the book – editors, producers, and news editors get tons of books. DOING THIS
•Develop a press release for newspaper reviews – have to include a copy of book DONE
•Target syndicated and national radio shows, i.e. Michael Baisden, XM radio, Tom Joyner
•Target radio shows in major markets like New York, Los Angeles, and Chicago that reach a large audience – we have to research what shows would be appropriate
•Seek out high profile, heavily attended workshops, for example, The Learning Annex, and The Mind Body Spirit shows - in Los Angeles these shows draw 30 -50,000 people over a weekend . It not then I would suggest that you create a video to: a – send to people that are looking for workshop events for their groups and b – to sell on my website and at other events.
•Develop a digital marketing campaign –
•create a story that will cause Yahoo, AOL, and AT&T news to pick up a story about Carol
•utilize the digital media, Facebook, Twitter, email lists to send out compelling messages and one liners from the book . DOING How does drawing a footprint on the side of your bed create a successful story for you? Thought provoking questions and ideas lead people to my website and gets them interested in the book
•Develop a marketing package to reach large women's groups.
•Register with speakers bureaus so that when people are looking for a speaker, they will see my bio and profile – I can sell books and hopefully videos at these events
• I want to sell 15 books a week at $17

SAMPLE PRESS RELEASE

Poise for the Runway of Your Life

Carol S. Batey Shows Readers How to Tap into Personal Power, Achieve Their Destiny

NASHVILLE, Tenn. – Foremost among advice given by Eastern and Western self-help gurus alike is the achievement of balance. For author Carol S. Batey, this implies the ability to pursue your life's destiny free of doubt, with self-confidence and a sound mind, trusting in a higher power to guide you through. In her new guidebook, *Poise for the Runway of Your Life* ( ), Batey chronicles the incredible fulfillment of her life's destiny as a professional model and shows how readers can learn to tap into their own internal power of intuition to discover the endless possibilities that lie in wait for them on the runway of their life.

Accessible and full of bright optimism, *Poise for the Runway of Your Life* shows readers how to recreate their own lives and find balance via Batey's own amazing journey from homemaker and mother of six children to professional model at the age of 51. Batey is the first to admit that she had her doubts, but by listening to her inner voice, to God, and believing in herself, she was able to completely transform her life and accomplish her dreams.

Poise for the Runway of Your Life instructs readers on how to position themselves, both mentally and physically, for their life's destiny through Batey's personal revelations and triumphs. Batey emphasizes that total poise is not determined by the successes of one's life, but by the ability to recover from moments of crisis, duress and transition. She writes:

Every desire starts within your soul as a thought. It is then radiated f rom the inside out through words and action. Balanced thoughts, words, and action create the power and movement within the universe f or your desires to manif est into your reality. For instance, if you are ready to make a mov toward attaining your desires and you allow doubt, f ear, or worry to distract you, you will lose your power. This is a result of allowing your thinking to sidetrack you, which ultimately throws you of f balance and of f track. Hold what you desire to create f or yourself in your mind's eye and within your soul. This is balance. ... You inherently possess the authority to make all the important decisions that determine your position on the runway of your lif e.

For dreamers in any season of their life, *Poise for the Runway of Your Life* will inspire the confidence and hope to tap into the power of their God and to reach for the stars.

Carol S. Batey became a professional model with Elite Lifestyle Model in Atlanta at the age of 51. She also teaches regional workshops for churches and women's organizations, and appears on local and internet radio programs. This is her second book, following *Parents Are Lif esavers* (Corwin Press, 1996) and *In Due Season: Destiny's Calling Your Soul* ( ).

Carol S. Batey,
615 485-4548

www.ingramcontent.com/pod-product-compliance
Lightning Source LLC
LaVergne TN
LVHW010103110826
845155LV00028B/459

* 9 7 8 1 9 3 5 3 2 3 1 0 5 *